Far East Business Chinese I

远东商务汉语 I

主编　叶德明 Yeh, Teh-Ming
编者　黄桂英 Huang, Jennifer Kuei-ying
　　　王文娟 Wang, Wen-chuan
　　　朱国华 Chu, Guo-hua

(Audio CD included)

远东图书公司

The Far East Book Co., Ltd.

Published by
The Far East Book Co., Ltd.
www.fareast.com.tw

North America Distributor
Elite Culture Educational Co.
www.eliteculture.com

ISBN 978-957-612-932-2

序

现代世界各地汉语学习已渐进入兴盛时代，基础汉语教材十分普遍，配合以中文为第二语言教学理论，提倡生活实际沟通、社会变迁、国际交流、文化传承的教材，也日渐趋向多元化的发展。

于此世界经济贸易互相往来交流之际，对商业界的洽谈与谘商交际，贸易股市的蓬勃交易，势必需求有关商业汉语专业术语表达的教材。

自2001年起，远东图书公司已陆续出版《远东生活华语》一系列的基本实用教材。并於国内海外广被读者选用，深受嘉许。

本书《远东商务汉语》响应国际趋势，配合时代潮流，进而在汉语学程上，提供内容更具生活化、实用化、功能化、具体化、经济与贸易文化之商业用语，以加强这方面的语文运用效能。

全套书共分三册，为初中级至中上级教材。第 I 册为初中级教材，乃是假设学习者已认识汉字两百个，词汇基础已认识五百条为起点。第 I 册十课，并加两课复习。第 II、III 册各十课。第 I 册汉字词汇增加至七百五十个，第 II 册扩展至一千，第 III 册达到一千三百个。并酌量增加工商文化方面之术语、俗语、专用名词等，期使外籍学习者能运用本套教材在正规学程中使用，并配合CD以供自学之用。

课文内容编辑如下：教学目标、经典佳句、场景对话、词语、词语练习、专有名词、重要句型、听力理解、阅读理解、你怎么说、工商文化智库等项目。

词汇标准以海峡两岸通行使用者为原则，为配合商场趋势，仍以中国大陆使用者为主，台湾流行者为辅，以达商业界沟通交际之功效。本教材由台湾师大国语教学中心王文娟、朱国华、黄桂英等三位老师共同编写。由台湾师大华语文教学研究所博士班学生李艾希（Ash Henson）翻译为英文。全书之用语经过香港教育学院中文系副教授张本楠博士审查指正，于此一并致谢。发行之後将广徵各方专家教师、学习者珍贵高见逐版改进以达完臻。

叶德明谨志

2010年6月

Preface

Everywhere in the modern world the study of Chinese has gradually entered a golden age. Learning materials for basic Chinese are widespread. In accordance with theory related to teaching Chinese as a second language, these materials recommend using Chinese in actual communication in daily life. Societal changes, international interaction and culture-inheriting language materials also tend to gradually develop in the direction of diversification.

In this time of global trade and economic exchange, business world negotiation and consultation as well as the frenzied interactions of a flourishing stock market, it is absolutely necessary to have language materials aimed at the technical terminology of the business world.

Since 2001, Far East Book Company has been publishing Far East Everyday Chinese, a series of practical and essential language materials, which have been widely acclaimed by readers both domestically and internationally.

Far East Business Chinese is a response to current global trends. Keeping with the times, it takes learning to the next level by providing content which is more practical, more functional, more concrete and more centered on daily life; in addition, it includes terminology found in financial and business cultures in order to augment language use in these areas.

This consists of 3 volumes containing lessons for basic-intermediate to advanced-intermediate students. The first volume is for basic-intermediate learners, suitable for those who have learned their first 200 Chinese characters and 500 vocabularies. The first volume has 10 lessons with additional 2 lessons for review. The second and third volumes each have 10 lessons. In the first and second volumes, the student will learn 250 new Chinese characters per volume, bringing their character vocabulary up to 750 characters and 1,000 characters respectively. In the third volume, the learner will reach the 1,300 character level. Furthermore, technical terms related to industry and commerce are covered as well as common vernacular and some specialized terminology. This set of books is meant to be used for standard Chinese courses and along with the included CD can also be used for self-study.

The course contents include the following: Learning Objectives, Common Phrases, Dialogue, Vocabulary, Vocabulary Exercises, Specialized Terms, Sentence Patterns, Listening Comprehension, Reading Comprehension, How Would You Say It, Business-Culture Knowledge Trove, etc.

The vocabulary in this course was chosen for its usefulness in both the People's Republic of China and in Taiwan, with emphasis on usage in the PRC, in order to achieve effective business communication and interaction. This course was created by three teachers from the Mandarin Training Center at National Taiwan Normal University (N.T.N.U), Wang, Wen-chuan, Chu, Guo-hua and Huang, Jennifer Kuei-ying. The English translation is by Ash Henson, a Ph.D. student in Teaching Chinese as a Second Language at N.T.N.U. Dr. Zhang Bennan of The Hong Kong Institute of Education proofread the entire course and provided some helpful insights. Opinions from specialists and students alike are most welcome to help us make future versions of this product even better.

Yeh, Teh-Ming

2010 / 06

目录
CONTENTS

请多指教

Nice to Meet You

1

Learning Objectives

When professionals meet for the first time, they usually introduce themselves by giving out their business cards. Business cards often give a lot of information about the person and the company they work for. The goals for this lesson are:

1. learn how to properly give someone your business card in a manner which is both polite and culturally appropriate
2. learn to understand the information which appears on business cards, including identifying what type of business a company does, the various positions within a company, etc.
3. learn how to describe your work

经典佳句 Common Phrases

这是我的名片，请多指教。
Zhè shì wǒ de míngpiàn, qǐng duō zhǐjiào.

请问，您在哪儿工作？
Qǐngwèn, nín zài nǎr gōngzuò?

我在公关部门负责对外联络的工作。
Wǒ zài gōngguān bùmén fùzé duìwài liánluò de gōngzuò.

场景对话 Dialogue (02)

王：您好，您贵姓？

李：我姓李，木子李，叫明，明天的明。
是工商日报的记者。您呢？

王：我姓王，叫大为。

李：王先生，您好，请问，您在哪儿工作？

王：日进贸易公司。这是我的名片。请多指教。

李：王经理。您好，很高兴认识您。
请问，您负责什么工作？

王：我在公关部门负责对外联络的工作。请多多指教。

李：哪里，哪里。不敢当。

王：希望以后我们能有机会合作。

日进贸易公司

公关部经理

王大为

地址：上海市南京路55号
电话：0086-592-290018
手机：13600901118
电子信箱：zhgd@rshtrde.com.cn

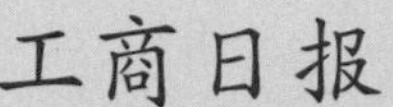

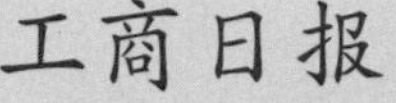

工商日报

记者

李 明

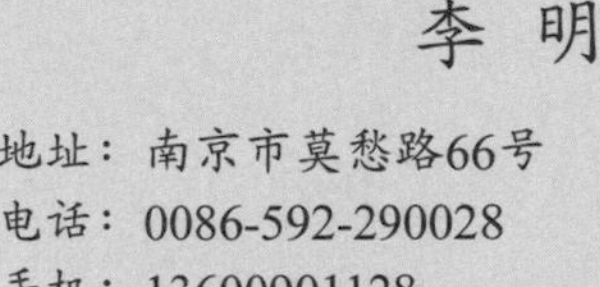

地址：南京市莫愁路66号
电话：0086-592-290028
手机：13600901128
电子信箱：lmr@gsnews.com.cn

Pinyin for Dialogue

Wáng:	Nín hǎo, nín guì xìng?
Lǐ:	Wǒ xìng Lǐ, mù zǐ lǐ, jiào Míng, míngtiān de míng. Shì Gōngshāng Rìbào de jìzhě. Nín ne?
Wáng:	Wǒ xìng Wáng, jiào Dàwéi.
Lǐ:	Wáng xiānsheng, nín hǎo, qǐng wèn, nín zài nǎr gōngzuò?
Wáng:	Rì Jìn Màoyì Gōngsī. Zhè shì wǒ de míngpiàn. Qǐng duō zhǐjiào.
Lǐ:	Wáng jīnglǐ. Nín hǎo, hěn gāoxìng rènshi nín. Qǐng wèn, nín fùzé shénme gōngzuò?
Wáng:	Wǒ zài gōngguān bùmén fùzé duìwài liánluò de gōngzuò. Qǐng duō duō zhǐjiào.
Lǐ:	Nǎlǐ, nǎlǐ. Bù gǎn dāng.
Wáng:	Xīwàng yǐhòu wǒmen néng yǒu jīhuì hézuò.

词语 Vocabulary (03)

Learn the Chinese characters and their pronunciations, then complete the writing assignment below.

记者	*N*	jìzhě	reporter
工作	*V/N*	gōngzuò	to work; a job (or jobs)
名片	*N*	míngpiàn	business card
指教	*N*	zhǐjiào	please give advice
经理	*N*	jīnglǐ	manager
认识	*V*	rènshi	to know
负责	*V*	fùzé	to be responsible for
公关	*N*	gōngguān	public relations
部门	*N*	bùmén	department
联络	*V*	liánluò	to contact
哪里	*IE*	nǎlǐ	Where? (In this lesson it's also used as polite way of turning down a compliment)
不敢当	*IE*	bù gǎn dāng	(I) don't dare accept (your compliment)
机会	*N*	jīhuì	chance, opportunity
合作	*V*	hézuò	to work together; to cooperate
职位	*N*	zhíwèi	position (within a company)
主任	*N*	zhǔrèn	director, chair

产品	*N*	chǎnpǐn	product
生产	*V*	shēngchǎn	to produce
采访	*V*	cǎifǎng	to interview; to gather news

主题词汇 Main Vocabulary

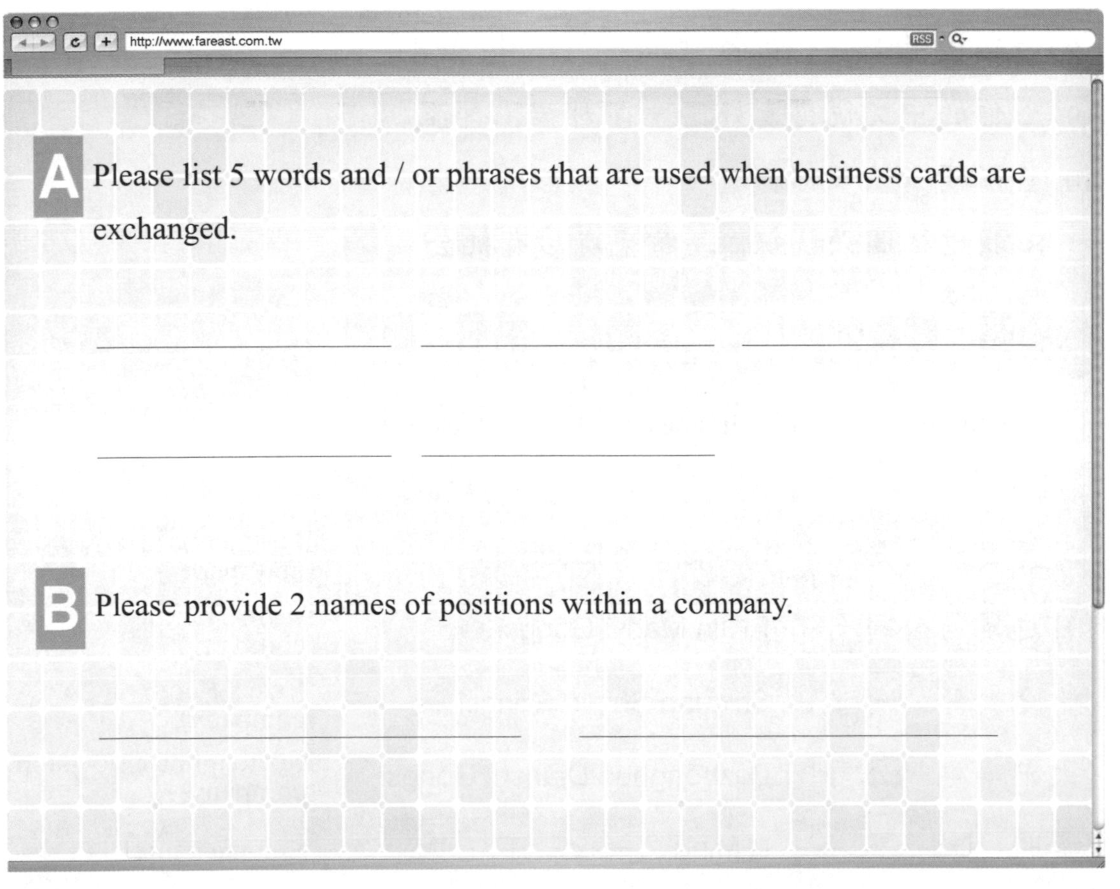

A Please list 5 words and / or phrases that are used when business cards are exchanged.

______________ ______________ ______________

______________ ______________

B Please provide 2 names of positions within a company.

______________ ______________

词语练习 Vocabulary Exercises

Use the words below to fill in the blanks.

联络　负责　工作　产品　指教　采访　生产　记者　合作　不敢当

1. 记者的工作是 __________ 新闻。
2. 这些新产品是哪一家公司 __________ 的？
3. 请问你在公司 __________ 什么工作？
4. 那家公司公关部门的经理，常跟记者 __________。
5. 很高兴认识你，请多 __________。
6. 请问，你在哪里 __________？
7. 他是工商日报的 __________。
8. 白经理说十全公司的 __________ 很有名。
9. A: 你的中文说得真好。　B: 那里，那里。__________。
10. A: 很高兴认识你。
    B: 我也很高兴认识你，希望以后有机会 __________。

专有名词 Specialized Terms (04)

Learn these specialized terms and complete the related exercises.

Terms	Pinyin	English
工商日报	Gōngshāng Rìbào	Commercial Daily (newspaper)
日进贸易公司	Rì Jìn Màoyì Gōngsī	Ri Jin Trading (company)
十全食品公司	Shíquán Shípǐn Gōngsī	Perfect Foods (company)
大中华电视公司	Dàzhōnghuá Diànshì Gōngsī	Dazhonghua Television (company)
李明	Lǐ Míng	person's name
王大为	Wáng Dàwéi	person's name

重要句型 Sentence Patterns

一、请多V

Normally used in polite speech indicating that the speaker wishes the listener to V, where V may be to help out, give advice, keep in touch, etc.

- 请多采访。
- 请多合作。

1. 请多 ____________。
2. 请多 ____________。

二、S在……部门负责……的工作

This sentence pattern emphasizes that a certain person at a certain department (within a company or work unit) does a certain type of work. The key here is to say the department name (of a certain company or work unit) first, and then describe the type of work. Under no circumstances is that order to be reversed.

- 他在贸易公司的公关部门负责联络的工作。
- 你在工商日报负责采访新闻的工作。

1. 张经理在食品公司负责 __________ 的工作。
2. 我在 ___________ 负责 __________ 的工作。

三、希望以后+Clause

This pattern is used to express the hope or expectation of the speaker towards the content of 'Clause'. However, it may also just be polite speech, especially when used meeting someone for the first time.

- 希望以后我们还有机会再见。
- 希望以后大家多合作。

1. 希望以后 _________________。
2. 希望以后 _________________。

听力理解 Listening Comprehension（05）

日进贸易公司

公关部经理

王大为

地址：上海市南京路55号
电话：0086-592-290018
手机：13600901118
电子信箱：zhgd@rshtrde.com.cn

工商日报

记者

李明

地址：南京市莫愁路66号
电话：0086-592-290028
手机：13600901128
电子信箱：lmr@gsnews.com.cn

（　）1. 李明是 ❶公关部经理 ❷工商日报的记者 ❸公关部主任。

（　）2. 李明负责 ❶采访新闻 ❷联络工作 ❸指教的工作。

（　）3. 王大为的职位是 ❶记者 ❷主任 ❸经理。

（　）4. 王大为负责 ❶采访新闻 ❷介绍的工作 ❸对外联络的工作。

大中华电视公司

新闻部主任 陈美芳

地址：广州市中山路48号
电话：0086-592-290038
手机：13600901138
电子信箱：cmf@chintv.com.cn

十全食品公司

生产部经理

白文文

地址：北京市成府路1082号
电话：0086-592-290048
手机：13600901148
电子信箱：wmj@yhoo.com.cn

（　）1. 陈主任在 ❶公关部 ❷生产部 ❸新闻部工作。

（　）2. 白经理在 ❶新闻部 ❷生产部 ❸公关部工作。

阅读理解 Reading Comprehension

张海是大中华电视公司新闻部的主任，他是上个周末认识王大为的，王大为是日进贸易公司公关部的经理。虽然王大为是英国人，可是他中文说得很好。他给张海名片的时候，说“请多指教”，还问张海在哪儿工作。张海觉得王大为的中文学得真好，所以他想下个星期要请一个记者去采访王大为是怎么学中文的。

(　　) 1. 张海的职位是 ❶记者 ❷经理 ❸主任

(　　) 2. 张海为什么要请记者去采访王大为，因为 ❶王大为是外国人 ❷王大为是经理 ❸王大为的中文学得真好

(　　) 3. 张海什么时候认识王大为？ ❶上个周末 ❷下个星期 ❸不知道

你怎么说? How Would You Say It?

( ) 1. 这是我的名片，	A 负责采访新闻的工作。
( ) 2. 请问你在哪里工作?	B 负责生产新产品。
( ) 3. 请多指教。	C 哪里，哪里。不敢当。
( ) 4. 记者	D 负责对外联络的工作。
( ) 5. 公关部经理	E 十全食品公司。
( ) 6. 生产部门	F 请多指教。

English Translation

Wang: Hello. And you are? *(Literally: What is your last name?)*

Li: I'm Miss Li. My first name is Ming, the Ming from míngtiān ('tomorrow'). I'm a reporter from Commercial Daily. And you?

Wang: I'm Mr. Wang. My first name is Dawei.

Li: Mr. Wang, nice to meet you *(Literally: How are you?)*. Where do you work?

Wang: Ri Jin Trading. Here's my card. Please feel free to give me any advice you may have. *(This is a polite phrase used to indicate that the speaker is less knowledgeable than the listener)*.

Li: Mr. Wang, how are you doing? It's nice to meet you. May I ask what type of work you do? *(Literally: what your work responsibilities are?)*

Wang: I'm a liaison for the public relations department. Please feel free to give me any advice you may have.

Li: You're too kind. *(This is a polite response to the phrase 请多多指教)*.

Wang: I hope that we will have the chance to work together sometime.

工商文化智库 Business-Culture Knowledge Trove

- When Chinese people meet for the first time, they usually exchange business cards. Business cards are offered by holding the card in both hands and bowing. At the same time, the person offering the card maintains eye contact and says "请多指教". The person accepting the card accepts it with both hands and says "哪里，哪里。不敢当。".
- Chinese people usually use a person's business title together with a last name to address someone, as in 王经理 ('manager Wang') or 李主任 ('director Li').
- "哪里，哪里。不敢当。" is the polite way to respond to a compliment and indicates humility.

Answer Key

主题词汇 Main Vocabulary

A. 名片、工作、指教、哪里、不敢当

B. 经理、主任

词语练习 Vocabulary Exercises

1. 采访 2. 生产 3. 负责 4. 联络 5. 指教
6. 工作 7. 记者 8. 产品 9. 不敢当 10. 合作

重要句型 Sentence Patterns

一、1. 指教
　　2. 帮忙

二、1. 生产
　　2. 电视公司；对外联络

三、1. 我们有机会合作
　　2. 我们可以常见面

听力理解 Listening Comprehension

一、1. ❷ 2. ❶ 3. ❸ 4. ❸

二、1. ❸ 2. ❷

阅读理解 Reading Comprehension

1. ❸ 2. ❸ 3. ❶

你怎么说? How Would You Say It?

1. F 2. E 3. C 4. A 5. D 6. B

接机 Picking up a Client from the Airport

2

Learning Objectives

Business people often need to pick up their clients from the airport. The goals for this lesson are related to meeting someone at the airport and include learning:

1. how to determine who you are supposed to be meeting and how to introduce yourself to them
2. how to greet your client(s) with the phrase 一路辛苦了 "You must be tired from your journey" (literally: it's been a hard journey) and to make sure that they have all their luggage
3. that clients are usually given a reception after being picked up from the airport
4. to plan a period of rest for your client(s) at their hotel before requiring them to attend any other activities

经典佳句 Common Phrases

我叫〇〇〇，代表〇〇公司来接您。
Wǒ jiào OOO, dàibiǎo OO Gōngsī lái jiē nín.

一路辛苦了。您的行李是不是都拿到了？
Yílù xīnkǔ le. Nín de xíngli shì bú shì dōu nádào le?

今天晚上总经理在北京楼给您接风。
Jīntiān wǎnshang zǒng jīnglǐ zài Běijīng Lóu gěi nín jiēfēng.

我先送您到饭店休息，六点半再来接您。
Wǒ xiān sòng nín dào fàndiàn xiūxi, liù diǎn bàn zài lái jiē nín.

场景对话 Dialogue (06)

李：请问，您是金安电脑公司的王经理吗？我叫李仁，代表中友科技公司来接您。

王：李先生，谢谢您来接我。这是我的名片，请多指教。

李：哪里，哪里。欢迎您到北京来，一切都顺利吧？

王：很顺利，飞机八点多从纽约起飞，航班准时到达，入关的时候也没问题。

李：一路辛苦了。您的行李是不是都拿到了？

王：拿到了，都在这儿。这个小礼物，请您收下。

李：您太客气了。今天晚上七点钟，我们总经理在北京楼给您接风。

王：谢谢您。我一来就麻烦大家，真不好意思。

李：别客气。那么，我先送您到饭店休息，六点半再来接您。

Pinyin for Dialogue

Lǐ:	Qǐng wèn, nín shì Jīn Ān Diànnǎo Gōngsī de Wáng jīnglǐ ma? Wǒ jiào Lǐ Rén, dàibiǎo Zhōng Yǒu Kējì Gōngsī lái jiē nín.
Wáng:	Lǐ xiānsheng, xièxie nín lái jiē wǒ. Zhè shì wǒ de míngpiàn, qǐng duō zhǐjiào.
Lǐ:	Nǎlǐ, nǎlǐ. Huānyíng nín dào Běijīng lái, yíqiè dōu shùnlì ba?
Wáng:	Hěn shùnlì, fēijī bā diǎn duō cóng Niǔyuē qǐfēi, hángbān zhǔnshí dàodá, rùguān de shíhou yě méi wèntí.
Lǐ:	Yílù xīnkǔ le. Nín de xíngli shì bú shì dōu nádào le?
Wáng:	Nádào le, dōu zài zhèr. Zhèi ge xiǎo lǐwù, qǐng nín shōuxià.
Lǐ:	Nín tài kèqi le. Jīntiān wǎnshang qī diǎn zhōng, wǒmen zǒng jīnglǐ zài Běijīng Lóu gěi nín jiēfēng.
Wáng:	Xièxie nín. Wǒ yì lái jiù máfan dàjiā, zhēn bùhǎoyìsi.
Lǐ:	Bié kèqi. Nàme, wǒ xiān sòng nín dào fàndiàn xiūxi, liù diǎn bàn zài lái jiē nín.

词语 Vocabulary (07)

Learn the Chinese characters and their pronunciations, then complete the writing assignment below.

机场	*N*	jīchǎng	airport
接机	*V*	jiējī	to meet someone at / pick up someone from the airport
代表	*V*	dàibiǎo	to represent
接	*V*	jiē	to meet (someone); to pick someone up
欢迎	*V*	huānyíng	to welcome
一切	*N*	yíqiè	everything
顺利	*SV*	shùnlì	smooth; without encountering problems
起飞	*V*	qǐfēi	to take off (said of aircraft)
航班	*N*	hángbān	(airline) flight
准时	*Adv*	zhǔnshí	to be on time, punctual
到达	*V*	dàodá	to reach or arrive at (a destination)
入关	*V*	rùguān	to enter customs (e.g. at an airport)
一路辛苦	*IE*	yílù xīnkǔ	a hard or difficult journey
行李	*N*	xíngli	luggage
收下	*V*	shōuxià	to accept or receive
总经理	*N*	zǒng jīnglǐ	general manager

接风	*V*	jiēfēng	to receive visitors
送	*V*	sòng	to take (someone to someplace); to escort
登机	*V*	dēngjī	to board (an airplane)

主题词汇 Main Vocabulary

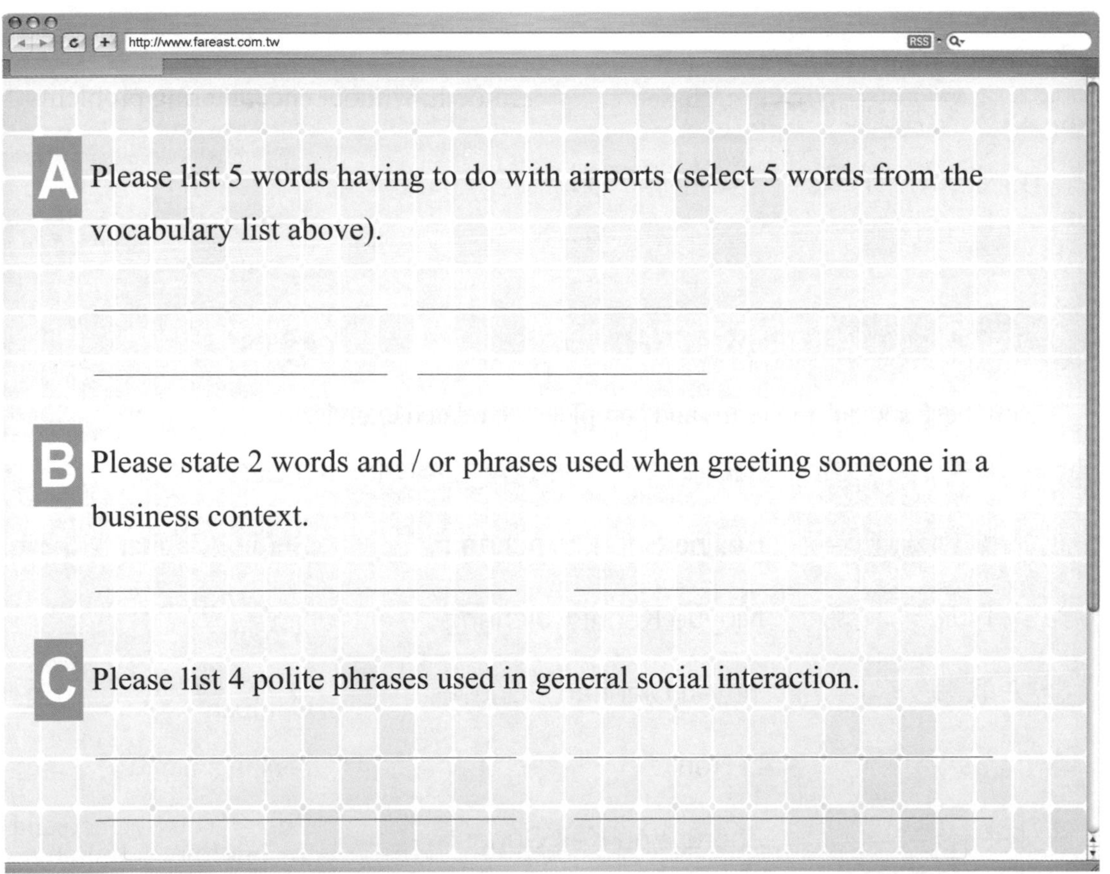

A Please list 5 words having to do with airports (select 5 words from the vocabulary list above).

______________________ ______________________ ______________________

______________________ ______________________

B Please state 2 words and / or phrases used when greeting someone in a business context.

______________________ ______________________

C Please list 4 polite phrases used in general social interaction.

______________________ ______________________

______________________ ______________________

词语练习 Vocabulary Exercises

Use the words below to fill in the blanks.

一路辛苦	接	行李	接机	起飞	到达	收下	接风

1. 我要到北京首都机场去 ________。
2. 李仁代表中友科技公司去 ________ 王经理。
3. 你坐的飞机是几点 ________ 的？
4. 王经理已经 ________ 北京了。
5. 总经理今天晚上要给谁 ________？
6. A: 这个小礼物请您 ________。
   B: 谢谢。您太客气了。
7. 下了飞机，别忘了拿 ________。
8. A: 欢迎您到北京来，________ 了。
   B: 哪里，哪里。一切都很顺利。

专有名词 Specialized Terms (08)

Learn these specialized terms and complete the related exercises.

Terms	Pinyin	English
北京首都机场	Běijīng Shǒudū Jīchǎng	Beijing Capital Airport
纽约肯尼迪机场	Niǔyuē Kěnnídí Jīchǎng	New York Kennedy Airport
金安电脑公司	Jīn Ān Diànnǎo Gōngsī	Jin An Computer Company
李仁	Lǐ Rén	person's name
中友科技公司	Zhōng Yǒu Kējì Gōngsī	Zhong You Science and Technology Company
北京楼	Běijīng Lóu	Peking Garden Restaurant

重要句型 Sentence Patterns

一、飞机 ______ 从 ______ 起飞，航班 ______ 到达
时间 / 地方 / 时间

This sentence pattern is used to explain what time a flight takes off, from where it is departing and what time it arrives at its destination. When emphasizing the departure location, place it before the takeoff time in the sentence. For example, "飞机从台北9点起飞，航班中午12点到达。

- 飞机8点多从纽约起飞，航班准时到达。
- 飞机下午3点半从台北起飞，航班5点10分到达。

1. 飞机上午10点5分从纽约起飞，航班 ______ 到达。
2. 飞机 ______ 从 ______ 起飞，航班 ______ 到达。

二、S_1先V_1O_1，(S_1) / S_2 再V_2O_2

This pattern expresses the order in which two actions occur, with the action of V_2 only occurring after the action of V_1 is complete. When the two actions are performed by different grammatical subjects, the second subject must be stated explicitly and must also appear before the second verb.

- 我先送您到饭店休息，6点半再来接您。
- 我先送总经理去机场，我们再回公司上班。

1. 我们先去北京楼吃饭，再 ______。
2. 主任先 ______，我们再 ______。

三、S_1一V_1O_1……(S_1) / S_2 就V_2O_2

This pattern expresses two actions which occur one right after the other. Sometimes the two actions are both performed by the same grammatical subject. When this is the case, the subject in the second clause may be left off; however, when the two actions are performed by different subjects, the subject in the second may not be left off and must also appear before the second verb.

- 我一来就麻烦大家，真不好意思。
- 王经理一到，我们就给他接风。

1. 工商日报的记者一到纽约就 ________________。
2. 总经理说：一 ____________________ 就要合作。

听力理解 Listening Comprehension（09）

1

（ ）1. 请问6点15分是

❶起飞的时间 ❷登机的时间 ❸到达的时间

2

（ ）1. 今天晚上请吃饭的人是

❶总经理 ❷白经理 ❸王大为

（ ）2. 在北京楼给您接风。是因为白经理

❶刚来 ❷要走 ❸飞机还没起飞

3

Below is a table of flight arrival times and departure times. Please fill in the table according to the information given in the audio.

航班	目的地	起飞时间	到达时间	登机口
CI 0912	纽约	6 : 20	9 : 45	______
AA 1203	北京	__ : __	2 : 36	32
CA 606	______	5 : 35	11 : 35	38

阅读理解 Reading Comprehension

金安电脑公司的王有为经理，上个星期五从纽约肯尼迪机场坐飞机到北京去，他坐的飞机是晚上8点零5分起飞的，飞机准时到达北京首都机场。李仁先生代表中友科技公司去接他。李先生先送王经理到饭店去休息，再接他去北京楼，因为晚上7点钟，中友科技公司的张总经理在那儿给王经理接风，欢迎他到北京来。

(　) 1. 王有为经理从哪里到哪里去?

❶从北京到纽约去 ❷从纽约到北京去 ❸从北京楼到纽约去

(　) 2. 李仁先生先去哪里?

❶北京首都机场 ❷北京楼 ❸饭店

(　) 3. 张总经理怎么欢迎王有为经理?

❶他去机场接王经理 ❷他请王经理吃饭

❸他送王经理去饭店休息

你怎么说? How Would You Say It?

( ) 1. 飞机几点到达?

( ) 2. 一切都很顺利吧?

( ) 3. 这个小礼物，请您收下。

( ) 4. 欢迎您来北京，

( ) 5. 您在哪个登机口登机?

( ) 6. 他一下飞机，

A 3号。

B 我们在北京楼给您接风。

C 谢谢，很好，没有问题。

D 就去北京楼。

E 您太客气了。

F 准时。

English Translation

Li: Excuse me, are you Mr. Wang, manager for the Jin An Computer Company? I'm Li Ren, representative for the Zhong You Science and Technology Company. I'm here to pick you up.

Wang: Mr. Li, thank you for coming to get me. Here's my card. Please feel free to give me any advice you may have *(This is a polite phrase used to indicate that the speaker is less knowledgeable than the listener)*.

Li: You're too kind. *(Literally: Where? Where? – This is a polite response to the phrase 请多指教)*. Welcome to Beijing. Did everything go smoothly?

Wang: Very smoothly. Our flight took off from New York after 8:00 and arrived on time. There were no problems going through customs either.

Li: You must be tired from your trip *(literally: a hard journey)*. Have you picked up all your luggage?

Wang: Yes. It's all here. Please accept this small gift.

Li: You're too kind *(literally: You're too polite)*. Tonight at 7:00, our general manager is holding a reception for you at the Peking Garden Restaurant.

Wang: Thank you. I just arrived and am putting everyone to so much trouble. I'm so embarrassed.

Li: Don't be so polite! OK, then. I'll take you to your hotel first so you can get some rest and then I'll be back at 6:30 to pick you up.

工商文化智库 Business-Culture Knowledge Trove

Receiving Guests and Business Culture

- In business, it is common to hold a reception for important customers after picking them up from the airport. In Chinese, this is called 接风 jiēfēng. After dinner, the reception is sometimes followed by activities such as going to a performance or going out to drink alcohol.
- When meeting someone who has just gotten off a long flight, we often say 一路辛苦了 *(meaning, 'it's been a hard journey')* to show our concern.

Answer Key

主题词汇 Main Vocabulary

A. 机场、接机、起飞、航班、入关、登机

B. 欢迎、一切顺利

C. 请多指教。您太客气了。一路辛苦了。
真不好意思。我一来就麻烦大家，真不好意思。

词语练习 Vocabulary Exercises

1. 接机　2. 接　3. 起飞　4. 到达　5. 接风
6. 收下　7. 行李　8. 一路辛苦

重要句型 Sentence Patterns

一、1. 准时 / 3点5分
2. 中午12点；北京；准时 / 6点15分

二、1. 到饭店休息
2. 联络王经理；去他的公司采访新闻

三、1. 马上联络王主任
2. 有机会

听力理解 Listening Comprehension

一、1. ❶　　二、1. ❶　2. ❶

三、26；10:30；上海

阅读理解 Reading Comprehension

1. ❷　2. ❶　3. ❷

你怎么说？ How Would You Say It?

1. F　2. C　3. E　4. B　5. A　6. D

上海饭店

The Shanghai Hotel

3

Learning Objectives

Business people often need to take clients out to eat.
The goals for this lesson are learning how to:

1. express gratitude. Sometimes it is necessary to seize an opportunity to make a tactful request.
2. introduce a restaurant's specialty dishes
3. understand the role of culinary culture in the Chinese business world

经典佳句 Common Phrases

这次我们对质量做了最高的要求。
Zhèi cì wǒmen duì zhìliàng zuòle zuì gāo de yāoqiú.

这家饭店的招牌菜是红烧鱼。
Zhèi jiā fàndiàn de zhāopaicài shì hóngshāo yú.

我们大家先干杯，吃了饭再谈吧！
Wǒmen dàjiā xiān gānbēi, chīle fàn zài tán ba!

场景对话 Dialogue（10）

吴经理：这次出货非常顺利，我代表公司谢谢贵厂各位领导。

孙厂长：谢谢！很高兴有机会再合作，这次我们对质量做了最高的要求。

吴经理：是啊！大家辛苦了。这家饭店的招牌菜是红烧鱼，我们来个鱼，还有醉鸡，怎么样？喝什么酒？

孙厂长：我们什么菜都喜欢吃，什么酒都喝，您点吧！

吴经理：吃招牌菜要喝好酒才行。服务员，来6瓶绍兴酒。

（点完菜）

孙厂长：吴经理，贵公司打算再订的5,000件，价钱方面可能要提高，因为有些原料涨价了。

吴经理：上菜了，我们大家先干杯，吃了饭再谈吧！

孙厂长：干杯。谢谢吴经理。希望吴经理多帮忙。

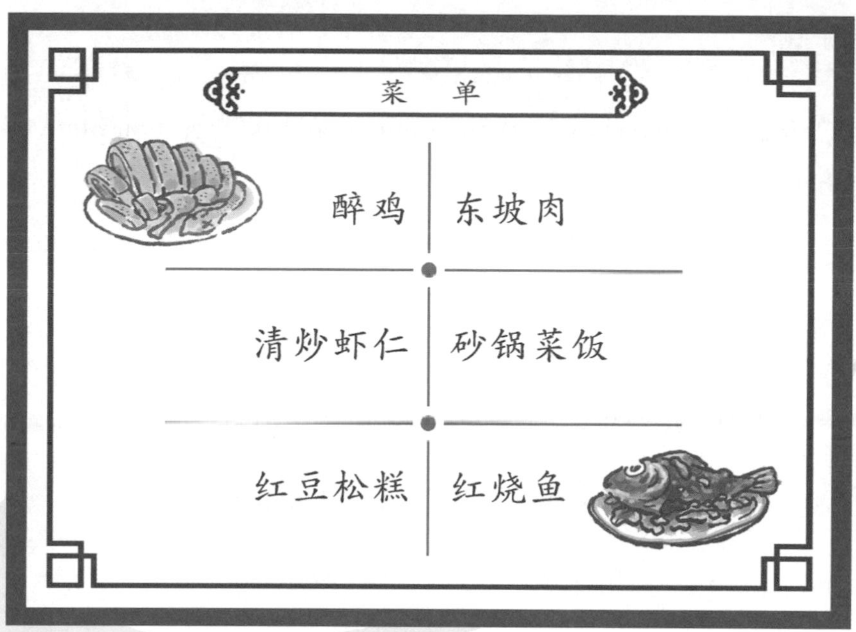

Pinyin for Dialogue

Wú jīnglǐ:	Zhèi cì chūhuò fēicháng shùnlì, wǒ dàibiǎo gōngsī xièxie guì chǎng gè wèi lǐngdǎo.
Sūn chǎngzhǎng:	Xièxie! Hěn gāoxìng yǒu jīhuì zài hézuò, zhèi cì wǒmen duì zhìliàng zuòle zuì gāo de yāoqiú.
Wú jīnglǐ:	Shì a! Dàjiā xīnkǔ le. Zhèi jiā fàndiàn de zhāopaicài shì hóngshāo yú, wǒmen lái ge yú, háiyǒu zuìjī, zěnmeyàng? Hē shénme jiǔ?
Sūn chǎngzhǎng:	Wǒmen shénme cài dōu xǐhuan chī, shénme jiǔ dōu hē, nín diǎn ba!
Wú jīnglǐ:	Chī zhāopaicài yào hē hǎo jiǔ cái xíng. Fúwùyuán, lái liù píng shàoxīng jiǔ.
(diǎnwán cài)	
Sūn chǎngzhǎng:	Wú jīnglǐ, guì gōngsī dǎsuàn zài dìng de wǔqiān jiàn, jiàqián fāngmiàn kěnéng yào tígāo, yīnwèi yǒuxiē yuánliào zhǎngjià le.
Wú jīnglǐ:	Shàng cài le, wǒmen dàjiā xiān gānbēi, chīle fàn zài tán ba!
Sūn chǎngzhǎng:	Gānbēi. Xièxie Wú jīnglǐ. Xīwàng Wú jīnglǐ duō bāngmáng.

词语 Vocabulary (11)

Learn the Chinese characters and their pronunciations, then complete the writing assignment below.

出货	*VO*	chū//huò	to produce or manufacture goods; to deliver goods
各	*Dem*	gè	each
领导	*N*	lǐngdǎo	leadership; guide
厂长	*N*	chǎngzhǎng	factory director
质量	*N*	zhìliàng	quality
要求	*N*	yāoqiú	requirement; request; demand
招牌菜	*N*	zhāopaicài	specialty (dish)
红烧	*V*	hóngshāo	to braise in soy sauce
醉	*SV*	zuì	drunk
点（菜）	*VO*	diǎn (cài)	to order (a dish)
行	*IE*	xíng	to be okay, to be acceptable
服务员	*N*	fúwùyuán	waiter; waitress; service person
订	*V*	dìng	to place an order (for merchandise)
价钱	*N*	jiàqián	price
方面	*N*	fāngmiàn	aspect

提高	*V*	tígāo	to raise; to increase
原料	*N*	yuánliào	raw material(s)
涨价	*VO*	zhǎngjià	to rise in price
上菜	*VO*	shàng//cài	to bring food to the table
干杯	*IE*	gānbēi	to dry one's glass (usually said when drinking alcohol)
谈	*V*	tán	to speak or chat about

主题词汇 Main Vocabulary

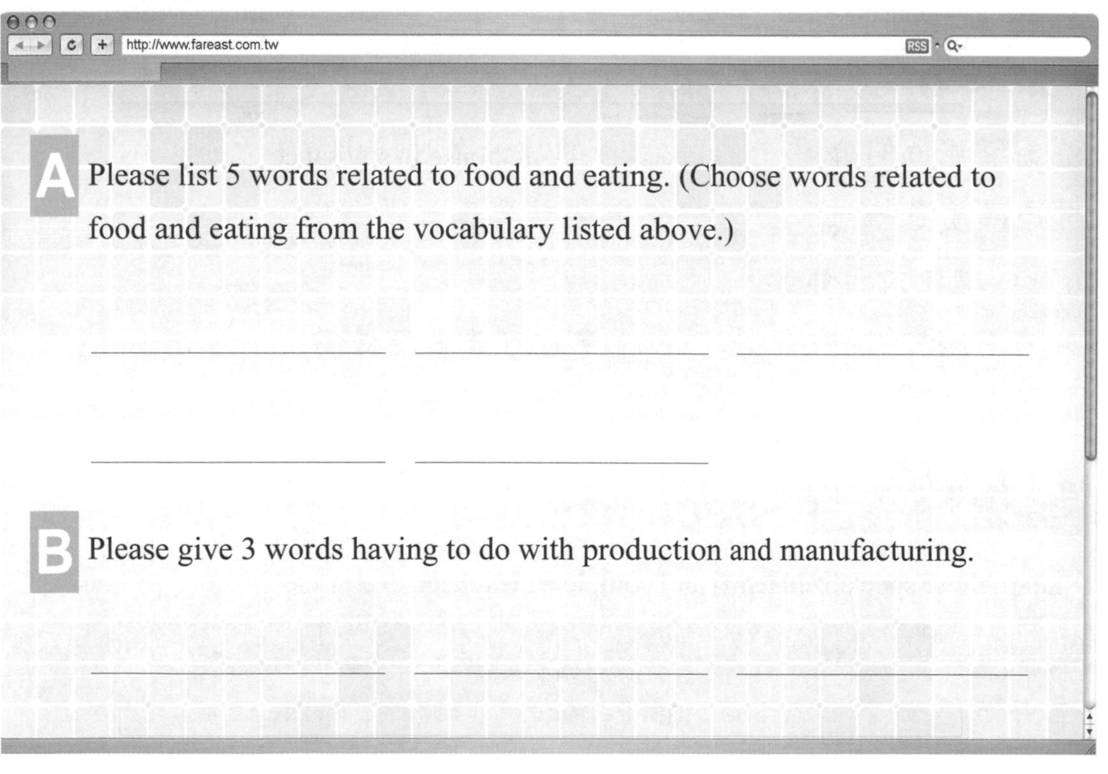

A Please list 5 words related to food and eating. (Choose words related to food and eating from the vocabulary listed above.)

______ ______ ______

______ ______

B Please give 3 words having to do with production and manufacturing.

______ ______ ______

词语练习 Vocabulary Exercises

Use the words below to fill in the blanks.

出货　要求　各　质量　点菜　订　提高　上菜　价钱　方面　原料
涨价　醉

1. 请问贵厂什么时间可以 __________？
2. 那家公司生产的产品 __________ 很好。
3. 厂长 __________ 产品得准时出货。
4. 我的中文不太好，还不会 __________，请您点吧！
5. __________ 国都有好吃的菜。
6. 厂长不会喝酒，一喝酒就 __________ 了。
7. A：那家饭馆的菜做得不错，可是 __________ 太慢了。

   B：是啊！我常常吃完第一个菜，第二个菜还没来。
8. 吴经理他们公司 __________ 的货什么时候出货？
9. 产品质量一 __________，客人就要再订。
10. A：现在东西都贵了。

    B：没错，价钱 __________ 了，可质量没提高。

专有名词 Specialized Terms (12)

Learn these specialized terms and complete the related exercises.

Terms	Pinyin	English
上海饭店	Shànghǎi Fàndiàn	The Shanghai Hotel

实用名词 Practical Vocabulary (12)

Learn the practical vocabulary and complete the related exercises.

Terms	Pinyin	English
上海菜	shànghǎi cài	Shanghainese Cuisine
绍兴酒	shàoxīng jiǔ	Shaoxing rice wine
红烧鱼	hóngshāo yú	red-braised fish
醉鸡	zuìjī	wine-steeped chicken (also called drunken chicken)

重要句型 Sentence Patterns

一、……方面

Anything in the shape of a cube has 6 sides or faces. When looking at such an object from different angles, you see its different faces. In a similar fashion, any given matter has its own scope and important aspects. As such, a speaker may use the term "……方面" 'aspect' *(literally: 'square face', like the face of a cube)* to limit the scope or point out a particular aspect of what they are saying.

- 价钱方面可能要提高，因为有些原料涨价了。
- 质量方面，公司应该做最大的要求。

1. 今天是我第一天上班，________ 方面请多指教。

2. 这一次到上海来，________ 方面都很顺利。

二、S什么O都V……

In order to express an idea which includes all members of a group, whether it be a group of people, matters or objects, the sentence pattern "QW……都……" is often used. That which follows "都" can be either an affirmative or negative sentence. For negative sentences, either "都" or "也" can be used taking the form "S什么……都/也 + negative sentence".

- 我们什么菜都喜欢吃，什么酒都喝。
- 小吴什么酒都/也不喝。
- 李：你吃饭了吗？
  王：我什么东西都没吃。

1. 孙经理在公司什么 ________ 都 ________，非常忙。

2. 王小姐什么 ________ 都 ________，可什么 ________ 也 ________。

3. 张经理请客的时候，吴厂长什么 ________ 也没 ________。

4. 小陈什么 ________ 都没 ________，所以大家都不知道他来了。

三、要……才……

This sentence pattern emphasizes that a certain method must be employed to uphold a given standard, obtain approval or meet a set of requirements. The sole condition which needs to be met appears before "才".

- 吃上海菜要喝绍兴酒才行。
- 出货要准时才好。

1. 别人说「请多指教」，我们要说 ________ 才 ________。

2. 价钱涨价了，质量方面要 ________ 才 ________。

四、来 + (Nu) + M + N

When ordering at a restaurant, this sentence pattern can be used to tell the server what is wanted and in what quantities. If only one of a given item is being ordered, then the number is sometimes left off. In this case, it's acceptable to just say the measure word and the desired menu item.

- 我们来个鱼，还有醉鸡，怎么样？
- 服务员，来6瓶绍兴酒。

1. 小吴爱喝酒，一进饭店就跟服务员说：「我先 ________，再点菜」。

2. 服务员，再 ________。

听力理解 Listening Comprehension（13）

①

（　）1. 请问北京楼的招牌菜是什么？

❶红烧鸡跟醉鱼 ❷醉鸡跟醉鱼 ❸醉鸡跟红烧鱼

（　）2. 请问北京楼的招牌菜跟上海饭店里有名的菜一样吗？

❶一样 ❷不一样 ❸有的一样，有的不一样

②

（　）1. 李经理觉得提高价钱行吗？

❶他没办法负责 ❷行 ❸不行

（　）2. 为什么价钱要提高？因为

❶要对质量做最高的要求 ❷要订货 ❸有些原料涨价了

阅读理解 Reading Comprehension

孙大明是十全公司负责出货的领导，他每天的工作都很忙，有的时候还要跟客人吃饭。昨天日进贸易公司的吴经理，请他们在上海饭店吃醉鸡跟红烧鱼，还喝了不少绍兴酒，要谢谢他们帮忙顺

利出货。吃饭的时候吴经理非常高兴，他跟孙大明说：“你们辛苦了，这次你们对质量做了最高的要求，出货也准时，我代表公司谢谢你们，大家干杯！”

( ) 1. 谁代表公司请吃饭？❶领导 ❷吴经理 ❸孙大明

( ) 2. 孙大明的工作是什么？❶吃饭 ❷出货 ❸贸易

( ) 3. 下面哪一句是对的？

❶孙大明这次顺利出货 ❷孙大明请吴经理吃上海菜

❸喝绍兴酒要干杯

你怎么说？How Would You Say It?

( ) 1. 辛苦了，干杯！ Ⓐ 不行，我醉了。

( ) 2. 原料涨价了， Ⓑ 我们来一个吧！

( ) 3. 这家饭馆的招牌菜是红烧鱼， Ⓒ 什么都行。

( ) 4. 多喝一点儿吧！ Ⓓ 可价钱方面太贵了。

( ) 5. 各位喜欢吃什么？ Ⓔ 干杯！

( ) 6. 那家公司的产品质量很好， Ⓕ 产品的价钱要提高才行。

English Translation

Mr. Wu (manager): Production went very smoothly this time. The company I represent would like to extend its thanks to your factory's leadership.

Mr. Sun (factory director): Thank you! I'm glad to have the opportunity to work together again. This time around, we employed the highest quality standards.

Mr. Wu (manager): That's right. Everyone put in a lot of work. The specialty here (at this restaurant) is the red-braised fish. Let's order the fish and the wine-steeped chicken. What do you think? What type of alcohol would you like?

Mr. Sun (factory director): We can eat and drink anything. Please go ahead and order (for us).

Mr. Wu (manager): When eating the specialty, you have to have the proper drinks! Waiter, please bring six bottles of Shaoxing rice wine.

(after ordering)

Mr. Sun (factory director): Mr. Wu *(literally: Manager Wu)*, your company is planning on ordering another 5,000 units. As far as the price, it might go up since the price of some of the raw materials has increased.

Mr. Wu (manager): The food is here. Let's all first empty our glasses. We can talk after we eat.

Mr. Sun (factory director): Bottoms up! Thank you Mr. Wu. I hope that we will be able to work more with you in the future. *(Literally: I hope that Mr. Wu will help more.)*

工商文化智库 Business-Culture Knowledge Trove

- Chinese dinning etiquette is very particular about seating arrangement. Traditional Chinese meals are served at a round table, although sometimes regular tables may be used. The seat facing the door is reserved for the guest of honor, while the seat facing the guest of honor is reserved for the host. The male and female hosts sit next to one another with the female host sitting to the right of the male host. The female guest of honor also sits next to and to the right of the male guest of honor. Other guests are seated in a male-female alternating pattern around the table.
- Some say that business in China is done by eating. That is to say, business is often conducted at restaurants, sitting around the table eating, talking business and drinking alcohol. When alcohol accompanies the meal, there are many calls to “dry” one’s glass, meaning to drink an entire glass in one breath. Drying one’s glass is seen as being respectful and showing earnestness.

Answer Key

主题词汇 Main Vocabulary

A. 点菜、招牌菜、红烧鱼、上菜、干杯、醉鸡

B. 质量、要求、价钱、订

词语练习 Vocabulary Exercises

1. 出货　2. 质量　3. 要求　4. 点菜　5. 各
6. 醉　7. 上菜　8. 订　9. 提高　10. 涨价

重要句型 Sentence Patterns

一、1. 工作
　　2. 各

二、1. 工作；做　　2. 菜；爱吃；菜；不会做
　　3. 价钱；跟张经理谈　　4. 人；联络

三、1. “不敢当”；客气
　　2. 提高；行

四、1. 来瓶酒
　　2. 来一杯茶

听力理解 Listening Comprehension

一、1. ❸　2. ❶

二、1. ❷　2. ❸

阅读理解 Reading Comprehension

1. ❷　2. ❷　3. ❶

你怎么说？ How Would You Say It?

1. E　2. F　3. B　4. A　5. C　6. D

Note

4 坐出租车

Taking a Taxi

Learning Objectives

China is a large country. Business people there travel all over and often need to take a taxi to reach their destination. The goals for this lesson are to learn:

1. the vocabulary related to taking a taxi
2. how to reach your destination
3. how the Chinese go about paying the bill

经典佳句 Common Phrases

坐地铁也行，打的也行。
Zuò dìtiě yě xíng, dǎdī yě xíng.

往前一直走，走到头，再往左拐。
Wǎng qián yìzhí zǒu, zǒudào tóu, zài wǎng zuǒ guǎi.

请直走，前面路口右拐。
Qǐng zhí zǒu, qiánmiàn lùkǒu yòu guǎi.

怎么能让客人付钱呢?
Zěnme néng ràng kèrén fùqián ne?

场景对话 Dialogue (14)

钱：今天是周末，我们去黄浦江跟外滩附近看看，怎么样?

张：好主意，我们怎么去?

钱：坐地铁也行，打的也行。那么就打车去国际会议中心吧!

（钱招手打车）

张：（上车对司机）师傅，请到国际会议中心。

钱：请先直走，到前面路口右拐，再往前一直走，走到头，然後再往左拐。

张：真不错，这儿的出租车不但车型统一，车况好，司机形象也好。

钱：可不，就像我们公司产品的质量一样，都是一流的。

张：是啊！这就是我们下单最重要的考量。

张：（拿钱给司机）师傅，请打发票。

钱：（不让张付钱）我付，我付，怎么能让您付钱呢?

Pinyin for Dialogue

Qián:	Jīntiān shì zhōumò, wǒmen qù Huángpǔ Jiāng gēn Wàitān fùjìn kànkan, zěnmeyàng?
Zhāng:	Hǎo zhǔyi, wǒmen zěnme qù?
Qián:	Zuò dìtiě yě xíng, dǎdī yě xíng. Nàme jiù dǎchē qù Guójì Huìyì Zhōngxīn ba! (Qián zhāoshǒu dǎchē)
Zhāng:	(shàng chē duì sījī) Shīfu, qǐng dào Guójì Huìyì Zhōngxīn.
Qián:	Qǐng xiān zhízǒu, dào qiánmiàn lùkǒu yòu guǎi, zài wǎng qián yìzhí zǒu, zǒudào tóu, ránhòu zài wǎng zuǒ guǎi.
Zhāng:	Zhēn búcuò, zhèr de chūzūchē búdàn chēxíng tǒngyī, chēkuàng hǎo, sījī xíngxiàng yě hǎo.
Qián:	Kěbù, jiù xiàng wǒmen gōngsī chǎnpǐn de zhìliàng yíyàng, dōu shì yīliú de.
Zhāng:	Shì a! Zhè jiùshì wǒmen xiàdān zuì zhòngyào de kǎoliang.
Zhāng:	(ná qián gěi sījī) Shīfu, qǐng dǎ fāpiào.
Qián:	(bú ràng Zhāng fùqián) Wǒ fù, wǒ fù, zěnme néng ràng nín fùqián ne?

词语 Vocabulary (15)

Learn the Chinese characters and their pronunciations, then complete the writing assignment below.

主意	*N*	zhǔyi	idea; plan
地铁	*N*	dìtiě	subway; metro
打的	*VO*	dǎdī	to take a taxi
打车	*VO*	dǎchē	to take a taxi
招手	*VO*	zhāo//shǒu	to wave one's hand(s)
司机	*N*	sījī	driver
师傅	*N*	shīfu	used to address service workers
拐	*V*	guǎi	to turn
出租车	*N*	chūzūchē	taxi
车型	*N*	chēxíng	model (of car)
统一	*SV*	tǒngyī	united
车况	*N*	chēkuàng	condition (of a vehicle)
形象	*N*	xíngxiàng	image
可不	*IE*	kěbù	Isn't it though?; That's right.
一流	*SV*	yīliú	first-rate; of the best quality
下单	*VO*	xià//dān	to place an order

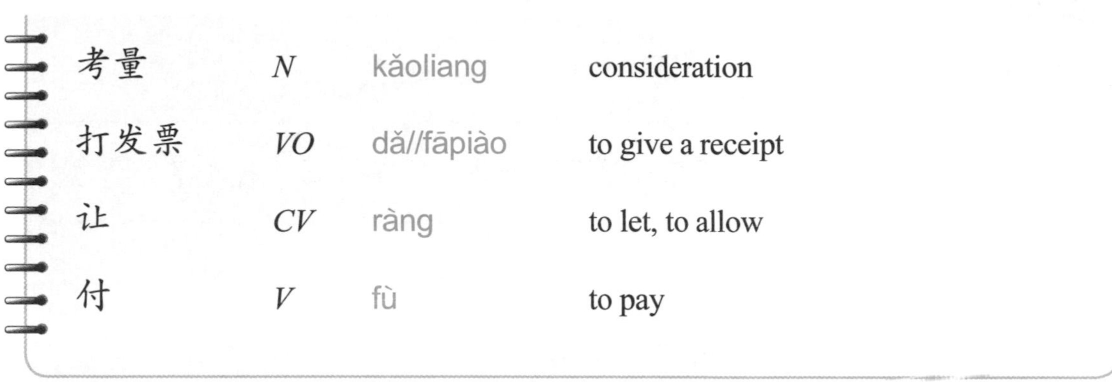

考量	*N*	kǎoliang	consideration
打发票	*VO*	dǎ//fāpiào	to give a receipt
让	*CV*	ràng	to let, to allow
付	*V*	fù	to pay

主题词汇 Main Vocabulary

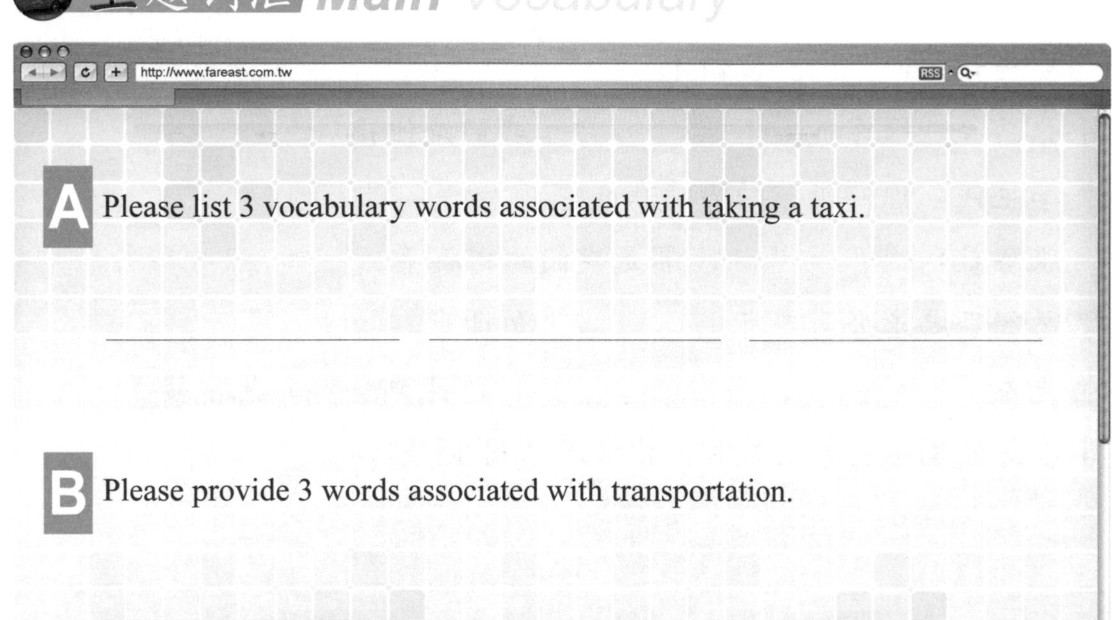

A Please list 3 vocabulary words associated with taking a taxi.

_______________ _______________ _______________

B Please provide 3 words associated with transportation.

_______________ _______________ _______________

词语练习 Vocabulary Exercises

Use the words below to fill in the blanks.

打的　出租车　车况　形象　可不　一流　下单　拐　打发票　让

1. 有些地方，晚上 ________ 车钱贵一点。
2. 张经理坐 ________ 去机场接客人。
3. 那辆车已经开了十年了，________ 好吗？
4. 十全公司的 ________ 很好，不但出货准时，产品质量也高。
5. 要价钱方面不涨，我们才 ________。
6. 张总经理很客气，不 ________ 我们给他接风。
7. 李主任：你们饭馆的醉鸡真好吃。
   服务员：________，那是我们的招牌菜。
8. 总经理要求公司要有 ________ 的干部。
9. 先左 ________，再右 ________，走到头就到北京楼了。
10. 在你的国家打的付钱时，出租车的司机 ________ 吗？

专有名词 Specialized Terms (16)

Learn these specialized terms and complete the related exercises.

Terms	Pinyin	English
国际会议中心	Guójì Huìyì Zhōngxīn	International Convention Center
黄浦江	Huángpǔ Jiāng	Huangpu River
外滩	Wàitān	the Bund

重要句型 Sentence Patterns

一、Q：……？ A：……也行，……也行。

This sentence pattern is usually used to express that both options are okay.

- 问："我们怎么去国际会议中心？"

  答："坐地铁也行，打的也行。"

- 问："经理说要点什么菜？"

  答："经理说点红烧鱼也行，醉鸡也行。"

1. 李：这次旅行你想到哪儿？

   王：去 ________ 也行，去 ________ 也行。

2. 钱总：谢主任觉得小王到哪个部门工作好？

   谢主任：要他负责 ________ 的工作也行，________ 的工作也行。

二、不但……也……

This sentence pattern expresses that the situation / conditions which follow 也 are included together with those that follow 不但. If the topic for the phrase following 也 is different from that which follows 不但, then it appears before 也. Otherwise it is omitted.

- 不但车型统一，车况好，司机形象也好。
- 这家公司不但出货准时，产品质量也高。

1. 小张在食品公司不但负责 ________，也要跟客人 ________。
2. 这家饭馆不但菜 ________，价钱也 ________。

三、就像NP一样

This sentence pattern is used to express the idea that some person, thing or matter is similar in some way to the NP within the pattern. The person, thing or matter may be directly stated before 就像, or be left off entirely.

- 就像我们公司产品的质量一样，都是一流的。
- 厂长要求出货准时，就像航空公司要求航班一样。

1. 钱小姐做的红烧鱼就像 ________ 一样。

2. 白主任的考量就像 ____________ 一样。

四、怎么能让……呢？

This pattern takes the form of a counter-question and is used to express that something which was previously stated is unreasonable and should not be allowed to happen.

- 怎么能让客人付钱呢？
- 怎么能让客人买了东西不付钱呢？

1. 接机怎么能让 ________ 等呢？

2. 怎么能让 ________ 再下单呢？

听力理解 Listening Comprehension (17)

( ) 1. 白主任今天要做什么？❶开车 ❷打电话 ❸到国际会议中心

( ) 2. 要怎么样白主任才放心？

❶车况不错 ❷一流的车 ❸司机放心

( ) 1. 李总经理觉得醉鸡怎么样？

❶好吃 ❷不好吃 ❸还没吃，不知道

(　) 2. 他们怎么到饭馆去？

❶坐地铁 ❷坐出租车 ❸坐地铁也行，打的也行

阅读理解 Reading Comprehension

黄浦江和外滩都是上海附近有名的地方，那里不但有好看的风景，也有很多一流的饭馆，从外国来的客人都喜欢去那里看看，吃吃上海菜。小钱是中友贸易公司的重要领导，常代表公司去黄浦江附近的国际会议中心开会，要是时间够，他就坐地铁去，要是没时间就打车。上个星期五，小钱要打的去国际会议中心的时候，看见一个外国人也想打的去外滩的一家饭馆，可是不知道怎么用中文跟司机说，小钱帮他告诉司机："师傅，这位外国朋友说，先往前一直走，走到头，再右拐，就到了"。

(　) 1. 黄浦江和外滩为什么有名？

❶有国际会议中心 ❷地方好看，菜好吃 ❸外国人都喜欢去

(　) 2. 小钱帮谁的忙？

❶他的外国朋友 ❷一个想打的的外国人

❸一个不知道饭馆在哪儿的外国人

(　) 3. 上个星期五，小钱为什么打的去国际会议中心？

❶要帮外国朋友的忙 ❷要告诉司机怎么走 ❸没时间坐地铁

你怎么说? How Would You Say It?

(　) 1. 一直往左走，	A 怎么能让你付钱呢。
(　) 2. 我请你吃上海菜，	B 这是下单的重要考量。
(　) 3. 国际会议中心到了。	C 坐地铁也行，打的也行。
(　) 4. 十全公司的产品质量很高。	D 走到头，再右拐。
(　) 5. 出货要求准时，	E 请打发票，谢谢！
(　) 6. 外滩怎么去?	F 可不，是一流的。

怎么走? How Do You Get There?

1. 工商日报记者小王，要去日进贸易公司，他要怎么走?

____

2. 你从大中华电视公司去地铁站，怎么走？

____

3. 李主任从地铁站到十全食品公司去，他要怎么走？

____

English Translation

Qian: Since it's the weekend *(literally: Today is a weekend day.)*, let's go down near the Huangpu River and the Bund and have a look around. What do you think?

Zhang: Good idea. How are we going to get there?

Qian: We can either take the metro or go by taxi. Let's just go ahead and take a cab to the International Convention Center.

(Qian hails a taxi.)

Zhang: *(To the driver when getting in the taxi)* Driver, to the International Convention Center, please.

Qian: Please go straight first. When you get to the intersection, turn right and keep going to the end of the road, then turn left.

Zhang: Not bad at all. The taxis here not only all look the same, but they are in good condition and the drivers project a good image *(literally: the driver(s)'s image is also good.)*

Qian: That's right. Just like our company's products *(literally: the quality of our company's products)*, which are all of first-rate.

Zhang: Right. That's the most important consideration for us when we place an order.

Zhang: *(While giving money to the driver)* Driver, can I get a receipt, please?

Qian: *(Not letting Zhang pay)* I got it. I got it. *(Literally: I'll pay. I'll pay.)* How could I possibly let you pay?

工商文化智库 Business-Culture Knowledge Trove

- When taking customers out, Chinese business people usually choose to take a taxi or to drive themselves. Taking a taxi is not only comfortable, but it is also a social courtesy and a way of showing respect to clients.
- Chinese people are very hospitable and as such, like to play host to show their sincerity. Because of this, Chinese people are often seen in social situations vying to pay the bill. It is not customary in China for everyone to pay for their own meal or to split the bill equally. When taking a taxi, the person paying sits behind the driver; even though one would normally sit up front when taking a taxi alone, since it's more convenient that way to pay the fare.
- Sometimes people sit next to the driver in order to show respect and equality, because sitting behind the driver can be seen as a way of putting on airs.
- Also, some people like to chat with the driver and that is more convenient from the front seat.

Answer Key

主题词汇 Main Vocabulary

A. 打的、打车、车型、车况、司机、
形象、招手、拐、打发票、付

B. 地铁、出租车、车型、车况、司机

词语练习 Vocabulary Exercises

1. 打的 2. 出租车 3. 车况 4. 形象 5. 下单
6. 让 7. 可不 8. 一流 9. 拐；拐 10. 打发票

重要句型 Sentence Patterns

一、1. 北京；上海
2. 采访；联络

二、1. 出货；联络
2. 好吃；不贵

三、1. 饭馆做的
2. 总经理的考量

四、1. 客人
2. 货先出

听力理解 Listening Comprehension

一、1. ❸ 2. ❶

二、1. ❶ 2. ❷

阅读理解 Reading Comprehension

1. ❷ 2. ❷ 3. ❸

Answer Key

你怎么说？How Would You Say It?

1. D　2. A　3. E　4. F　5. B　6. C

怎么走？How Do You Get There?

1. 他要往西一直走，到第二个路口就是日进贸易公司了。
2. 我得往南走，到第二个路口左拐，再往前一直走，地铁站就在路口。
3. 李主任要往北一直走，下两个路口左拐就到了。

出差

Taking a Business Trip

5

Learning Objectives

Business people often need to travel to conduct business.
The goals for this lesson are to:

1. understand the purpose of business travel
2. learn how to plan a travel itinerary
3. learn the role a secretary plays when the person in charge is on travel

经典佳句 Common Phrases

这是〇〇〇，请您过目。
Zhè shì OOO, qǐng nín guòmù.

有你帮忙真好，要不然我就忙不过来了。
Yǒu nǐ bāngmáng zhēn hǎo, yàobùrán wǒ jiù máng bú guòlái le.

谢谢夸奖，这是我应该做的。
Xièxie kuājiǎng, zhè shì wǒ yīnggāi zuò de.

场景对话 Dialogue (18)

秘　　书：陈总，下个星期您到南方出差的行程，我都安排好了。这是行程表，请您过目。

陈总经理：有你帮忙真好，要不然我就忙不过来了。

秘　　书：谢谢夸奖，这是我应该做的。陈总觉得这样的安排可以吗？

陈总经理：行。这次除了要看分公司的业务，还要拜访武汉、重庆、广州的客户，了解市场上对我们产品的反应。

秘　　书：那我先准备产品的资料，再联络客户。

陈总经理：对了，另外请帮我整理要拜访的客户名片，我得带着。

秘　　书：好的，要通知分公司的人接机吗？

陈总经理：不用了，请他们到饭店来就行了。

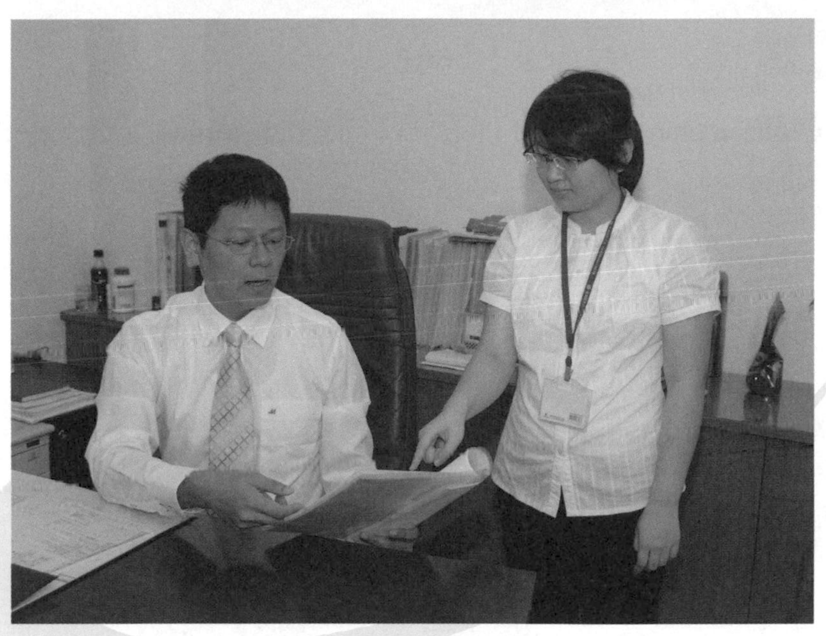

Pinyin for Dialogue

mìshū:	Chén zǒng, xià ge xīngqī nín dào nánfāng chūchāi de xíngchéng, wǒ dōu ānpái hǎo le. Zhè shì xíngchéngbiǎo, qǐng nín guòmù.
Chén zǒngjīnglǐ:	Yǒu nǐ bāngmáng zhēn hǎo, yàobùrán wǒ jiù máng bú guòlái le.
mìshū:	Xièxie kuājiǎng, zhè shì wǒ yīnggāi zuò de. Chén zǒng juéde zhèyàng de ānpái kěyǐ ma?
Chén zǒngjīnglǐ:	Xíng. Zhèi cì chúle yào kàn fēngōngsī de yèwù, hái yào bàifǎng Wǔhàn, Chóngqìng, Guǎngzhōu de kèhù, liǎojiě shìchǎng shàng duì wǒmen chǎnpǐn de fǎnyìng.
mìshū:	Nà wǒ xiān zhǔnbèi chǎnpǐn de zīliào, zài liánluò kèhù.
Chén zǒngjīnglǐ:	Duìle, lìngwài qǐng bāng wǒ zhěnglǐ yào bàifǎng de kèhù míngpiàn, wǒ děi dàizhe.
mìshū:	Hǎode, yào tōngzhī fēngōngsī de rén jiējī ma?
Chén zǒngjīnglǐ:	Búyòng le, qǐng tāmen dào fàndiàn lái jiù xíng le.

词语 Vocabulary (19)

Learn the Chinese characters and their pronunciations, then complete the writing assignment below.

秘书	*N*	mìshū	secretary; office assistant
出差	*VO*	chūchāi	to go on business travel
行程	*N*	xíngchéng	travel itinerary
安排	*V/N*	ānpái	to arrange; plan
表	*N*	biǎo	table, list
过目	*V*	guòmù	to take a look at
要不然	*Adv*	yàobùrán	otherwise
忙不过来	*RC*	máng bú guòlái	to be too busy to handle
夸奖	*N*	kuājiǎng	to praise
分公司	*N*	fēngōngsī	branch office
业务	*N*	yèwù	professional work; business
拜访	*V*	bàifǎng	to visit; to call on
客户	*N*	kèhù	customer; client
了解	*V*	liǎojiě	to understand
反应	*N*	fǎnyìng	reaction
对了	*IE*	duìle	Oh, that's right.; correct, right

另外	*Adv*	lìngwài	in addition; also
整理	*V*	zhěnglǐ	to arrange, to put in order
带	*V*	dài	to take
通知	*V*	tōngzhī	to inform

主题词汇 Main Vocabulary

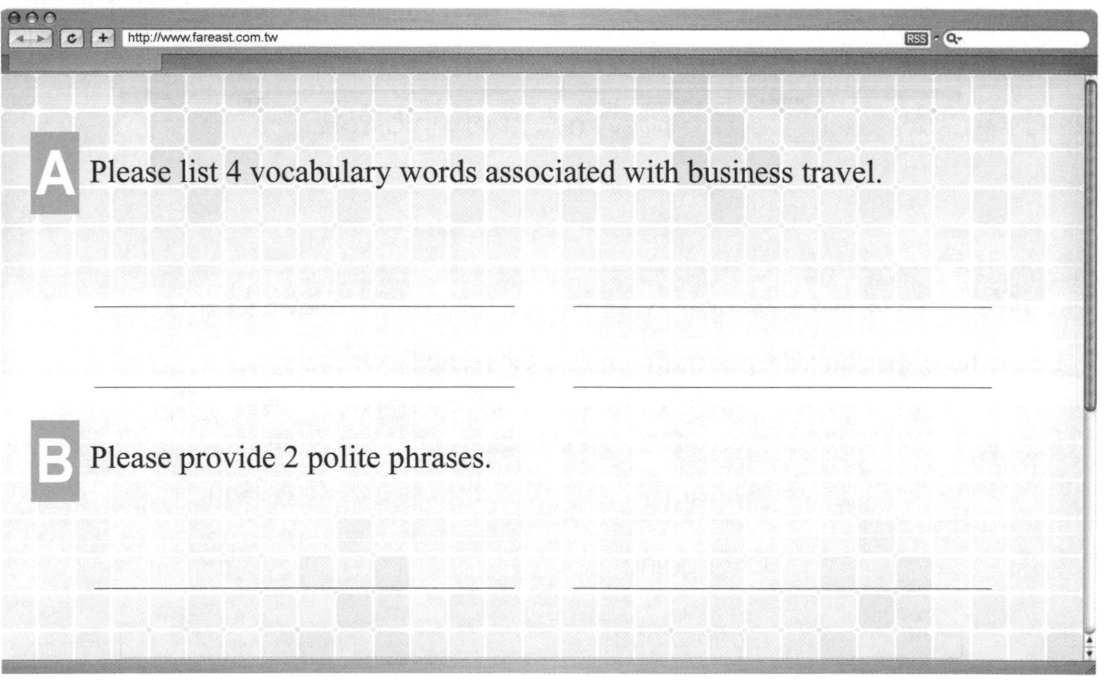

A Please list 4 vocabulary words associated with business travel.

______________________ ______________________

______________________ ______________________

B Please provide 2 polite phrases.

______________________ ______________________

词语练习 Vocabulary Exercises

Use the words below to fill in the blanks.

业务　反应　过目　通知　整理　客户　安排　要不然　另外　忙不过来

1. 这是航班表，请您 ________。
2. 去国际会议中心，坐地铁很方便，________ 打的也行。
3. 小陈什么事都得做，真的 ________，我们帮帮他吧！
4. 公关部门的 ________，有一些是联络的工作。
5. 张经理常代表公司去机场接 ________。
6. 价钱涨了，客人什么 ________ 都有。
7. 孙厂长叫小王 ________ 出货时间。
8. 吴主任点了这家饭馆的招牌菜，________ 还叫服务员拿了两瓶绍兴酒。
9. 旅行以前得先 ________ 行李。
10. 小李，去 ________ 司机，6点准时到北京楼。

专有名词 Specialized Terms (20)

Learn these specialized terms and complete the related exercises.

Terms	Pinyin	English
武汉	Wǔhàn	city name
重庆	Chóngqìng	city name
广州	Guǎngzhōu	city name

重要句型 Sentence Patterns

一、要不然……

"要不然" is used to connect two possible situations. If the first one doesn't occur, then the second one will.

- 有你帮忙真好，要不然我就忙不过来了。
- 价钱不能涨，要不然客户不下单。

1. 航班要准时，要不然得 ________。

2. 最好有人接机，要不然就得 ________ 了。

二、除了……还……

This pattern is used to express that "in addition to" the people, things or affairs which follow 除了, "but also" the people, things or affairs which follow 还.

- 除了要看分公司的业务，还要拜访武汉、重庆、广州的客户。
- 这家饭馆的招牌菜，除了醉鸡还有红烧鱼。

1. 要是希望公司形象好，除了要 ________ 还得 ________。

2. 出差以前除了要 ________ 还要 ________。

三、……上

Here, the meaning of 上 is "aspect(s)." So, "……上" means "aspect(s)," not "above."

- 了解市场上对我们产品的反应。
- 产品的质量上，我们做了最高的要求。

1. ________ 上，您觉得这样的安排怎么样？

2. 业务上，____________________。

四、V着

When 着 follows a verb, it indicates that the action of the verb is continuous.

- 要拜访的客户名片，我得带着。
- 厂长拿着产品给客户介绍。

1. 小钱 ________ 行程表去找主任了。

2. 中国人常在饭馆里 ________ 酒谈生意。

听力理解 Listening Comprehension (21)

1

(　) 1. 这次出差怎么样？ ❶还有问题 ❷一切顺利 ❸一路辛苦

(　) 2. 谁夸奖秘书？ ❶男的 ❷女的 ❸两人都夸奖

2

This is the travel itinerary for Mr. Lec, the general manager. Please fill in the chart according to what you hear.

行程 日期 / 时间	8/15	8/16	8/17	8/18	8/19
7:00					离开上海
			坐飞机去上海	拜访客户	
10:00					

				请日进贸易公司吴总吃饭	
2:30					
3:30					
4:00		跟中友贸易公司谈合作的事			

阅读理解 Reading Comprehension

吴总经理有两个秘书，王秘书负责安排吴总的一切行程，有的时候王秘书忙不过来，就请李秘书帮忙。吴总常给外国客人接风，要是有外国记者采访，吴总也要代表公司说话。吴总每个月最少出两次差，除了到各分公司去看业务，还要拜访客户，了解产品在市场上的反应。最近原料价钱涨了，各分公司的经理都说客户不想下单，所以吴总常常出差，还好有两个秘书一块儿合作，要不然吴总还真不知道该怎么办。

(　) 1. 为什么吴总最近常出差？因为

❶有两个秘书一块儿合作 ❷原料价钱涨了 ❸客户不下单

(　)2. 秘书不负责安排什么？

❶吴总请客的时间 ❷吴总跟记者说什么话 ❸吴总出差的行程

(　)3. 吴总为什么要到各分公司去？

❶了解各分公司经理做了什么事 ❷了解市场上对产品的反应

❸拜访客户

你怎么说？ How Would You Say It?

(　)1. 请秘书通知孙厂长出货，　Ⓐ 请您过目。

(　)2. 客人都夸奖你们产品的质量。　Ⓑ 对了，另外通知司机要接机。

(　)3. 今天除了要整理产品价钱表，　Ⓒ 要不然还不能采访。

(　)4. 王秘书，你的行程安排得真好。　Ⓓ 这是我们应该做的。

(　)5. 还好你带着名片，　Ⓔ 还要整理客户资料。

(　)6. 这是出货时间表，　Ⓕ 谢谢您的夸奖。

English Translation

Secretary: Mr. Chen, *(literally: General manager Chen)* I've already completed your travel itinerary for your trip down south next week. Here it is. Please take a look at it.

Mr. Chen: It's great having you around to help out. Otherwise, I'd be way too busy to handle everything.

Secretary: Thank you. *(Literally: Thanks for the praise.)* I'm just doing my job. *(Literally: This is what I should do.)* Mr. Chen, are the travel arrangements acceptable?

Mr. Chen: Yes, they are. *(Literally: Acceptable.)* For this trip, in addition to seeing how the branch office is doing, I'm going to visit our customers in Wuhan, Chongqing, and Guangzhou to get a better understanding of the market reaction to our products.

Secretary: In that case, I'll prepare the product information first and then contact the customers.

Mr. Chen: Oh, that's right. Can you also get together the name cards of the customers I'm going to visit? I need to take them with me.

Secretary: OK. Should I have someone from the branch office meet your flight?

Mr. Chen: That's not necessary. Just have them stop by the hotel.

工商文化智库 Business-Culture Knowledge Trove

- When Chinese people go on business travel, if their travel schedule isn't too tight and there is some free time available, some people take the opportunity to visit local cultural or scenic spots, such as the Yellow Crane Tower of Wuhan, the City God Temple (also called the Chenghuang Temple) of Shanghai, Beijing's Temple of Heaven or the Forbidden City, etc.

Answer Key

主题词汇 Main Vocabulary

A. 行程、整理、分公司、安排、行程表、拜访、客户、通知

B. 请您过目、谢谢夸奖、这是我应该做的

词语练习 Vocabulary Exercises

1. 过目　2. 要不然　3. 忙不过来　4. 业务　5. 客户
6. 反应　7. 安排　8. 另外　9. 整理　10. 通知

重要句型 Sentence Patterns

一、1. 通知客人
　　2. 坐出租车

二、1. 出货准时；产品质量好
　　2. 安排行程；整理行李

三、1. 行程
　　2. 我们希望有机会合作

四、1. 带着
　　2. 喝着

听力理解 Listening Comprehension

一、1. ❷　2. ❸

二、

行程 日期 时间	8/15	8/16	8/17	8/18	8/19
7:00					离开上海
9:00			坐飞机去上海	拜访客户	
10:00		拜访客户			
12:00				请日进贸易公司吴总吃饭	
2:30			去上海分公司看业务		
3:30	到广州分公司				
4:00		跟中友贸易公司谈合作的事			

阅读理解 Reading Comprehension

1. ❸　2. ❷　3. ❶

你怎么说？How Would You Say It?

1. B　2. D　3. E　4. F　5. C　6. A

听力理解 Listening Comprehension (22)

①

( ) 1. 下面哪一句是对的?

❶ 因为钱总接机，男的觉得不好意思，所以请大家吃饭。

❷ 男的觉得钱总跟领导来接机很麻烦。

❸ 钱总跟领导不但接机也请他们吃饭。

②

( ) 1. 谁整理名片?

❶小吴 ❷说话的男人 ❸小吴跟说话的男人

( ) 2. 为什么要整理名片?

❶小吴要出差 ❷小吴有时间 ❸小吴要联络

③

( ) 1. 为什么出货要准时?

❶产品质量好 ❷市场上的反应 ❸公司形象好

( ) 2. 为什么要提高公司形象?

❶客户能放心下单 ❷要对质量做最高的要求

❸客户的反应

④

( ) 1. 北方有中友公司的分公司吗?

❶只有北京有 ❷有不少 ❸没有

( ) 2. 中友公司总经理怎么知道领导做好工作没有？

❶出差到各分公司去看 ❷不但电话联络，也出差去看

❸各分公司领导自己负责

5

( ) 1. 谁希望快一点儿？

❶女的 ❷男的 ❸客户

( ) 2. 为什么希望要快一点儿？因为

❶第一次去机场 ❷他有他的考量 ❸心里急

( ) 3. 说话的这两个人是谁？

❶总经理和客户 ❷客人和出租车司机 ❸代表公司的人和客人

你怎么说？How Would You Say It?

( ) 1. 晚上6点半我们在北京楼给您接风。

( ) 2. 谢谢你帮忙整理，

( ) 3. 什么都涨价了。

( ) 4. 他们点的是这家饭馆的招牌菜。

( ) 5. 这儿的出租车是一流的，

A 是吗？我们也来一个吧！

B 先直走，到前面路口再右拐。

C 可不，不但好吃也好看。

D 我一来就麻烦你们，真不好意思。

E 别客气，您什么时候要来，就通知我们。

(　) 6. 小陈做的醉鸡就像上海饭店的招牌菜一样。
(　) 7. 李秘书什么方面都安排好了。
(　) 8. 这是出货表，请您过目。
(　) 9. 希望以后能有机会拜访贵公司。
(　) 10. 到国际会议中心怎么走？

F 时间上，全友公司订的8,000件，可能要再做考量。
G 不但车况好，司机形象也好。
H 有他帮忙真好，要不然我真忙不过来。
I 要不然行李太多，小吴忙不过来。
J 可不，从原料到产品都贵了。

阅读理解 Reading Comprehension

（一）

王明是纽约时报的记者，他上个月从纽约坐飞机到上海去，飞机准时到达上海浦东国际机场，他一下飞机，就打的到洋洋商务酒店去。

第二天早上，王明吃了早饭就走路去国际会议中心采访新闻，因为酒店离国际会议中心很近。走路，不但可以看黄浦江，也可以看外滩的大楼，他觉得外滩的大楼就像纽约的一样。走着走着，前面有一位小姐跟他招手，王明想了想那不是白文吗？白文是上海工商日报的记者。他们是去年在广州采访新闻的时候认识的。

他们在街上谈了一会儿话，就决定晚上6:30一起在外滩附近的上海饭馆吃饭，那天白小姐要付钱，但是王明说："怎么能让小姐请客呢？"白小姐只好听王明的话了。

(　) 1. 王明一到达上海就

❶和白文一块儿吃饭 ❷打的去商务酒店 ❸去国际会议中心

(　) 2. 王明为什么要走路去国际会议中心?

❶他想看白文 ❷酒店离国际会议中心不远

❸他要在附近吃早饭

(　) 3. 王明和白文是在 ❶纽约 ❷上海 ❸广州　认识的。

(　) 4. 王明出差到上海去

❶采访新闻 ❷看白文 ❸看黄浦江和外滩的大楼

(　) 5. 那天晚上吃饭，谁付钱?

❶白文 ❷王明 ❸两人一块儿付钱

（二）

我认识小钱十几年了，他在全友公司生产部门负责出货。全友公司的业务很大，从吃的、穿的到玩的、用的，什么都生产，进了全友公司的生产部门，就像进了市场一样。全友公司不但在中国各地都有分公司，美国、加拿大也有。客户都说全友公司形象好，除了产品质量一流，价钱不贵，出货还非常准时，让他们能放心下单。也因为这样，领导常夸奖小钱，出货时间安排得好，要不然各分公司的业务就麻烦了。我想公司一定要给小钱高一点儿的职位，多一点儿钱才行，可公司方面没什么反应。

( ) 1. 为什么领导常夸奖小钱？因为他

❶让客户放心下单 ❷在公司工作十几年了

❸负责的业务做得好

( ) 2. 全友公司的业务是什么？

❶出货 ❷生产 ❸市场

( ) 3. 为什么说全友公司像市场一样？

❶价钱不贵 ❷各地都有分公司 ❸什么产品都有

( ) 4. 客户觉得全友公司怎么样？

❶有一流的形象 ❷应该给小钱高职位

❸各分公司的业务很麻烦

( ) 5. 我觉得公司方面对小钱怎么样？

❶不够好 ❷没什么反应 ❸常夸奖小钱

短文写作 Short Essay

Please write an essay of 150 or more characters according to the order of the pictures below.

Reference vocabulary and sentence patterns for the short essay assignment:

出差行程表、名片、工作、指教、机场、接机、起飞、航班、入关、登机、点菜、招牌菜、红烧鱼、上菜、干杯、醉鸡

S在 ________ 负责 ________ 的工作

S_1先V_1O_1，（S_1）/ S_2 再V_2O_2

S_1一V_1O_1……（S_1）/ S_2 就V_2O_2

要……，才……

听力理解 Listening Comprehension

一、1. ❸

二、1. ❸ 2. ❸

三、1. ❸ 2. ❶

四、1. ❶ 2. ❷

五、1. ❶ 2. ❸ 3. ❷

你怎么说? How Would You Say It?

1. D 2. I 3. J 4. A 5. G

6. C 7. H 8. F 9. E 10. B

阅读理解 Reading Comprehension

（一）

1. ❷ 2. ❷ 3. ❸ 4. ❶ 5. ❷

（二）

1. ❸ 2. ❷ 3. ❸ 4. ❶ 5. ❶

短文写作 Short Essay

（略）

电话订房

Booking a Hotel Room by Phone

6

Learning Objectives

Since China is such a large country, business trips often require booking a hotel room. The goals for this lesson are to:

1. learn how to book a room over the phone
2. become familiar with the things you need to remember when booking a room
3. become familiar with hotel facilities and related safety issues

经典佳句 Common Phrases

下午好。这里是〇〇〇，很高兴为您服务。
Xiàwǔ hǎo. Zhèlǐ shì OOO, hěn gāoxìng wèi nín fúwù.

包括服务费和早饭吗？
Bāokuò fúwùfèi hé zǎofàn ma?

请稍候。
Qǐng shāohòu.

您的电话号码、信用卡号方便传真给我们吗？
Nín de diànhuà hàomǎ, xìnyòngkǎ hào fāngbiàn chuánzhēn gěi wǒmen ma?

场景对话 Dialogue (23)

林利：下午好，这里是里洋商务酒店，我是前台林利，很高兴为您服务。

胡思：你好！请问房间一个晚上多少钱？另外，我也想知道房间里有网络吗？

林利：好的，单人间的价钱是600元，双人间是900元。房间里都可以免费上网。

胡思：包括服务费和早饭吗？还有，可以打几折？

林利：包括早饭，可是服务费另外算。至于折扣，得看您什么时候入住？住几天？

胡思：我打算三月一号到，五号退房。要一个双人间，一个单人间。对了，房间请安排在安全门附近。

林利：好的，请稍候。噢，这段时间可以给您打九折。请问贵姓大名？您的电话号码、信用卡号方便传真给我们吗？

胡思：行，没问题。如果要取消订房的话，我一星期以前通知你们。

Pinyin for Dialogue

Lín Lì:	Xiàwǔ hǎo, zhèlǐ shì Lǐyáng Shāngwù Jiǔdiàn, wǒ shì qiántái Lín Lì, hěn gāoxìng wèi nín fúwù.
Hú Sī:	Nǐ hǎo! Qǐng wèn fángjiān yí ge wǎnshang duōshao qián? Lìngwài, wǒ yě xiǎng zhīdao fángjiān li yǒu wǎngluò ma?
Lín Lì:	Hǎode, dānrénjiān de jiàqián shì liù bǎi yuán, shuāngrénjiān shì jiǔ bǎi yuán. Fángjiān li dōu kěyǐ miǎnfèi shàngwǎng.
Hú Sī:	Bāokuò fúwùfèi hé zǎofàn ma? Háiyǒu, kěyǐ dǎ jǐ zhé?
Lín Lì:	Bāokuò zǎofàn, kěshì fúwùfèi lìngwài suàn. Zhìyú zhékòu, děikàn nín shénme shíhou rùzhù? Zhù jǐ tiān?
Hú Sī:	Wǒ dǎsuàn sān yuè yī hào dào, wǔ hào tuìfáng. Yào yí ge shuāngrénjiān, yí ge dānrénjiān. Duìle, fángjiān qǐng ānpái zài ānquánmén fùjìn.
Lín Lì:	Hǎode. Qǐng shāohòu. Òu, zhèi duàn shíjiān kěyǐ gěi nín dǎ jiǔ zhé. Qǐngwèn guìxìng dàmíng? Nín de diànhuà hàomǎ, xìnyòngkǎ hào fāngbiàn chuánzhēn gěi wǒmen ma?
Hú Sī:	Xíng, méi wèntí. Rúguǒ yào qǔxiāo dìngfáng dehuà, wǒ yì xīngqī yǐqián tōngzhī nǐmen.

词语 Vocabulary (24)

Learn the Chinese characters and their pronunciations, then complete the writing assignment below.

订房	*VO*	dìng//fáng	to book or reserve a room
前台	*N*	qiántái	front desk
网络	*N*	wǎngluò	the Internet

单人间	*N*	dānrénjiān	single room
元	*N*	yuán	unit of money
双人间	*N*	shuāngrénjiān	double room
免费	*Adv*	miǎnfèi	free of charge
上网	*VO*	shàng//wǎng	to get on-line; to get on the Internet
包括	*V*	bāokuò	to include
服务费	*N*	fúwùfèi	service fee
打折	*VO*	dǎ//zhé	to give a discount
算	*V*	suàn	to calculate
至于	*Conj*	zhìyú	as far as; concerning; to go as far as to
折扣	*N*	zhékòu	discount
入住	*V*	rùzhù	to check in (to a hotel room, etc.)
退房	*VO*	tuì//fáng	to check out (of a hotel room, etc.)
安全门	*N*	ānquánmén	safety exit
请稍候	*IE*	qǐng shāohòu	Please wait a moment.
段	*M*	duàn	period (of time); section
信用卡	*N*	xìnyòngkǎ	credit card
传真	*V*	chuánzhēn	to fax
取消	*V*	qǔxiāo	to cancel

主题词汇 Main Vocabulary

http://www.fareast.com.tw

A Please provide 5 words that might be used when booking a hotel room.

__________ __________ __________

__________ __________

B Please list 3 words related to lodging.

__________ __________ __________

词语练习 Vocabulary Exercises

Use the words below to fill in the blanks.

包括　段　算　打折　免费　取消　传真　上网　入住　折扣

1. 这家酒店有__________机场接送的服务。
2. 要是贵公司在九月三十号以前下单，我们就给您__________九__________。
3. 现在网络很方便，__________叫出租车也行。
4. 我们合作这么多年了，价钱方面可以给一些__________吧！
5. 如果酒钱也__________的话，这桌上海菜要一千元。

6. 里洋商务酒店的房间价钱 __________ 早饭。
7. 这些资料整理好，就可以 __________ 给客户了。
8. 如果 __________ 的时间还没到的话，行李可以先放在前台。
9. 因为总经理忙不过来，所以明天的行程 __________ 了。
10. 胡总出差的这 __________ 时间，公司业务是谁负责的？

专有名词 Specialized Terms (25)

Learn these specialized terms and complete the related exercises.

Terms	Pinyin	English
里洋商务酒店	Lǐyáng Shāngwù Jiǔdiàn	hotel name
林利	Lín Lì	person's name
胡思	Hú Sī	person's name

重要句型 Sentence Patterns

一、至于

至于 is used to connect two sentences which have different topics.

- 服务费另外算。至于折扣，得看您什么时候入住。
- 房间价钱包括早饭，至于服务费要另外算。

1. 李：他们工厂产品的价钱和质量怎么样？

   王：产品的质量是一流的，至于 ______________________。

2. 经理："客户很高兴，要再下单，问我们能不能早一点出货？"

   厂长："客户要下单，太好了，至于 ______________________。"

二、得看……

The matter described in this type of sentence is determined by the condition appearing after 看.

- 至于折扣方面，得看您什么时候入住？住几天？
- 吃饭的时候要喝什么酒，得看点什么菜。

1. 我们下单不下单，得看贵公司 ______________。
2. 你负责什么业务，得看 ______________。

三、如果……的话

The meaning of this sentence pattern is the same as that of 如果 and 要是. 如果 and 的话 can either be used together or one of them can be omitted.

- 如果要取消订房的话，我一星期以前通知你们。
- 如果一切顺利的话，三月十五号可以出货。

1. 如果天气不好，航班取消的话，______________。
2. 如果想去外滩附近看看的话，______________。

听力理解 Listening Comprehension（26）

（　）1. 客人希望什么？

❶房间价钱包括早饭 ❷在房间吃早饭

❸服务员让他下楼吃早饭

(　) 2. 服务员为什么要客人另外付服务费？

❶客人不舒服，不能下楼 ❷房间价钱不包括早饭

❸客人希望早饭送到房间

(　) 1. 一共几个人出差？ ❶一个 ❷两个 ❸三个

(　) 2. 下面哪一个不是秘书小姐订房的考量？

❶坐车方不方便 ❷有没有折扣 ❸能不能上网

First listen to the following conversation. Then look at the room prices below and help the manager by filling out the room reservation form.

How should Ms. Wang (the secretary) make the room reservation for the general manager?

里洋饭店从3月1号到3月31号的房间价钱表

	3/1-3/5	3/6-3/10	3/11-3/20	3/21-3/24	3/25-3/31
单人间	$675	$712	$750	$637	$735
双人间	$675	$712	$750	$637	$735

目的地： 1、

入住日期： 2、 月 日

入住晚数： 3、

退房日期： 4、 月 日

房间数量： 5、

房间类型： 6、 □ 单人间

□ 双人间

確定

阅读理解 Reading Comprehension

最近不但北京、上海有很多外国公司的分公司，重庆、武汉、广州也有不少了，所以各地都有商务酒店，方便生意人出差的时候住一段时间。这些商务酒店的服务都是一流的，要不然客人住一次，下次就不来了。至于价钱上，除了包括早饭，常常还有折扣，一定要让客人来了还想再来才行。另外，因为希望提高形象，免费上网和机场接送，也是酒店的重要考量。

(　) 1. 为什么各地都有商务酒店了？因为

❶有很多外国公司 ❷方便生意人出差 ❸希望提高酒店形象

(　) 2. 哪些主意酒店觉得能让他们形象好，下面哪个不对？

❶机场接送服务 ❷价钱上打折 ❸免费上网

(　) 3. 酒店怎么知道客人的反应？下面哪个不对？

❶客人来了还想再来 ❷客人住一次，下次就不来了

❸免费上网服务

你怎么说？How Would You Say It?

( ) 1. 我找胡主任听电话。	A 得看您用哪一种信用卡。
( ) 2. 可以打几折？	B 早饭免费，服务费另外算。
( ) 3. 包括服务费和早饭吗？	C 很高兴为您服务。
( ) 4. 酒店方便安排在外滩附近吗？	D 不包括早饭和服务费，900元。
( ) 5. 这里是工商日报，	E 好的，请稍候。
( ) 6. 双人间住一晚多少钱？	F 行，没问题。

English Translation

Lin Li: Good afternoon. This is the Liyang Business Hotel. This is Lin Li at the front desk *(literally: This is front desk Lin Li)*. Glad to be at your service.

Hu Si: Hello! How much does a room cost per night? Also, I would like to know if internet access is available in the rooms.

Lin Li: OK. Single rooms are 600 Yuan and double rooms are 900 Yuan. All the rooms have internet access.

Hu Si: Does that include service fees and breakfast? And can I get a discount?

Lin Li: Breakfast is included, but service fees are extra. As far as getting a discount, I need to know when you will be arriving and how long you will be staying.

Hu Si: I'm planning on arriving the first of March and checking out on the fifth. I would like one single room and one double room. Oh, yeah. Please make sure the rooms are near a safety exit.

Lin Li: OK. Please wait a moment. Hm. For those dates *(literally: This time period)*, I can give you a 10% discount. What is your name, please? And would it be convenient to fax us your phone number and credit card number?

Hu Si: OK. That's no problem. If I need to cancel the reservation, I'll notify you a week in advance.

工商文化智库 Business-Culture Knowledge Trove

- China is a large country. Guests houses which provide food and lodging were already in existence during the Shang Dynasty, but the word 旅馆 'hotel' only appeared during the Tang Dynasty. Though the names changed with the dynasties, the aim providing guests with multifaceted and comprehensive service has not changed. There are many types of Chinese hotels to choose from, depending on their size, quality of the facilities, and of course price, including 大酒店 dà jiǔdiàn (hotel), 大饭店 dà fàndiàn (hotel), 商务酒店 shāngwù jiǔdiàn (business-oriented hotel), 温泉饭店 wēnquán fàndiàn (hot spring hotel), 客栈 kèzhàn (inn), 宾馆 bīnguǎn (guesthouse), 汽车旅馆 qìchē lǚguǎn (motel), 旅店 lǚdiàn (tavern), 会馆 huìguǎn (lodge hotel), 公寓 gōngyù (hotel apartment), 民宿 mínsù (hostel) and 旅社 lǚshè (hostel).

Answer Key

主题词汇 Main Vocabulary

A. 订房、网络、折扣、服务费、信用卡、单人间、双人间

B. 入住、退房、打折、取消、安全门

词语练习 Vocabulary Exercises

1. 免费　2. 打（九）折　3. 上网　4. 折扣　5. 算

6. 包括　7. 传真　8. 入住　9. 取消　10. 段

重要句型 Sentence Patterns

一、1. 价钱（方面），就贵了

2. 出货（的时间），得再安排

二、1. 产品的价钱涨不涨

2. 在哪个部门工作

三、1. 就得通知客人

2. 坐地铁也行，打的也行

听力理解 Listening Comprehension

一、1. ❷　2. ❸

二、1. ❷　2. ❸

三、1. 广州　2. 3/21　3. 6晚　4. 3/27　5. 2间

6. 1个单人间和1个双人间

Answer Key

阅读理解 Reading Comprehension

1. ❷ 2. ❷ 3. ❸

你怎么说？How Would You Say It?

1. E 2. A 3. B 4. F 5. C 6. D

7 交际应酬

Entertaining Clients

Learning Objectives

When doing business, Chinese people pay special attention to etiquette, the giving and receiving of courtesies as well as the entertaining of guests. The goals for this lesson are to learn:

1. how to entertain business clients
2. how to use entertainment to maintain relationships with clients
3. how to use entertainment to build relationships with new clients

经典佳句 Common Phrases

这是怎么回事？
Zhè shì zěnme huíshì?

预算就这么多，这边费用增加了，别的地方就得减少了。
Yùsuàn jiù zhème duō, zhèi biān fèiyong zēngjiā le, biéde dìfang jiù děi jiǎnshǎo le.

可以再研究研究。
Kěyǐ zài yánjiū yánjiu.

请您指示。
Qǐng nín zhǐshì.

场景对话 Dialogue (27)

杨：胡经理，预算表上的交际费用比以前多，这是怎么回事？

胡：报告总经理，这是因为业务部门提高了端午节、中秋节和春节采购礼品的费用。

杨：为了跟客户的业务联络更顺利，除了吃饭应酬，过年过节也要送礼。可预算就这么多，这边费用增加了，别的地方就得减少了。

胡：我们公司最近想要跟深圳的一些“三资企业”合作，所以需要送礼的新客户增加了十几个。

杨：和新客户建立关系是正确的，不过，是不是一定要提高采购礼品的费用，可以再研究研究。

胡：请您指示。

杨：我想给旧客户送礼还是像以前一样，至于新客户，得看他们下多少单，再决定送什么礼。

胡：是的，我这就通知业务部门。

Pinyin for Dialogue

Yáng:	Hú jīnglǐ, yùsuànbiǎo shang de jiāojì fèiyong bǐ yǐqián duō, zhè shì zěnme huíshì?
Hú:	Bàogào zǒngjīnglǐ, zhè shì yīnwèi yèwù bùmén tígāole Duānwǔ Jié, Zhōngqiū Jié hé Chūn Jié cǎigòu lǐpǐn de fèiyong.
Yáng:	Wèile gēn kèhù de yèwù liánluò gèng shùnlì, chúle chīfàn yìngchou, guònián-guòjié yě yào sòng lǐ. Kě yùsuàn jiù zhème duō, zhèi biān fèiyong zēngjiā le, biéde dìfang jiù děi jiǎnshǎo le.
Hú:	Wǒmen gōngsī zuìjìn xiǎng yào gēn Shēnzhèn de yìxiē "sānzī qǐyè" hézuò, suǒyǐ xūyào sòng lǐ de xīn kèhù zēngjiāle shíjǐ ge.
Yáng:	Hé xīn kèhù jiànlì guānxi shì zhèngquè de, búguò, shì bú shì yídìng yào tígāo cǎigòu lǐpǐn de fèiyong, kěyǐ zài yánjiū yánjiu.
Hú:	Qǐng nín zhǐshì.
Yáng:	Wǒ xiǎng gěi jiù kèhù sòng lǐ háishi xiàng yǐqián yíyàng, zhìyú xīn kèhù, děi kàn tāmen xià duōshao dān, zài juédìng sòng shénme lǐ.
Hú:	Shìde, wǒ zhè jiù tōngzhī yèwù bùmén.

词语 Vocabulary (28)

Learn the Chinese characters and their pronunciations, then complete the writing assignment below.

预算	*N*	yùsuàn	budget
交际	*N*	jiāojì	social interaction
费用	*N*	fèiyong	fee; cost; expense
比	*CV*	bǐ	compared to

报告	*V*	bàogào	to report
采购	*V*	cǎigòu	to purchase
礼品	*N*	lǐpǐn	gift; present
为了	*CV*	wèile	for; in order to
更	*Adv*	gèng	still; yet; more
应酬	*V*	yìngchou	to entertain (guests)
过	*V*	guò	to celebrate (usually used with Chinese New Year, major festivals and birthdays)
送礼	*VO*	sòng//lǐ	to give a gift
增加	*V*	zēngjiā	to increase
减少	*V*	jiǎnshǎo	to decrease
需要	*V*	xūyào	to need; to want; to require
建立	*V*	jiànlì	to establish
正确	*SV*	zhèngquè	correct; accurate
不过	*Conj*	búguò	however
研究	*V*	yánjiū	to discuss; to think over
指示	*V*	zhǐshì	to point out
决定	*V*	juédìng	to decide

主题词汇 Main Vocabulary

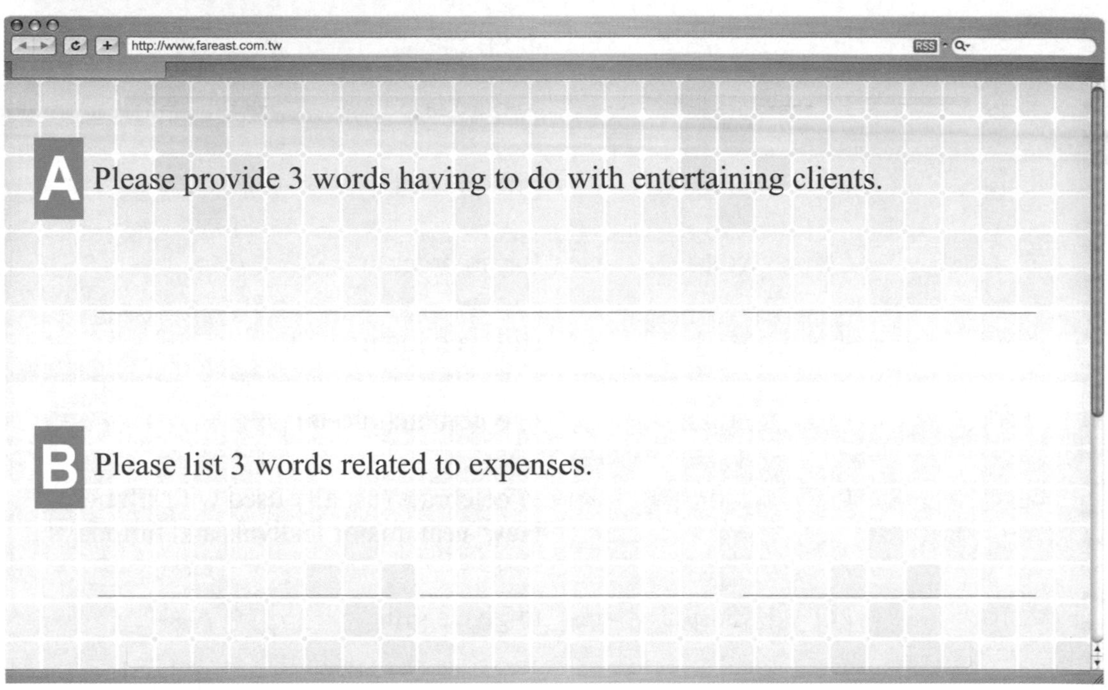

词语练习 Vocabulary Exercises

Use the words below to fill in the blanks.

决定　礼品　预算　采购　应酬　增加　研究　费用　正确　更

1. 商务酒店可以上网，联络客户 ________ 方便了。
2. 总经理，这是 ________ 表，请您过目。
3. 酒和茶常常是中国人送礼的 ________。
4. 公关部门的业务，除了对外联络，也包含和客人吃饭 ________。
5. 酒店前台说，机场接送的 ________ 要另外算。
6. 我们什么菜都吃，点什么，您 ________ 吧！

7. ____________ 多少钱的东西，得看预算有多少。

8. 美国飞中国的航班 ____________ 了，从美国到中国更方便了。

9. 领导让小陈 ____________ 怎么减少交际费用。

10. 经理的指示很 ____________。

专有名词 Specialized Terms (29)

Learn these specialized terms and complete the related exercises.

Terms	Pinyin	English
深圳	Shēnzhèn	city in Southern China

实用名词 Practical Vocabulary (29)

Learn the practical vocabulary and complete the related exercises.

Terms	Pinyin	English
端午节	Duānwǔ Jié	Dragon Boat Festival
中秋节	Zhōngqiū Jié	Mid-Autumn Festival
春节	Chūn Jié	Spring Festival
三资企业	sānzī qǐyè	Refers to the three types of companies which are funded or operated according to one of the three ways foreign investment and foreign management are allowed in China under Chinese law, namely: 1. Chinese-foreign equity joint ventures, 2. Chinese-foreign contractual joint ventures or 3. wholly foreign-owned enterprises.

重要句型 Sentence Patterns

一、N_1 比 N_2 SV

SV is the result of the comparison between N_1 and N_2.

- 预算表上的交际费用比以前多。
- 双人间的价钱比单人间贵。

1. 今年采购礼品的预算比去年 ________。

2. 深圳分公司的业务比广州分公司 ________。

二、为了……

That which appears after 为了 is a goal or objective. Following the goal or objective is an explanation of the method or means for obtaining it.

- 为了跟客户的业务联络更顺利，除了吃饭应酬，过年过节也要送礼。
- 为了下个月出差，小钱在商务酒店订了一个单人间。

1. 为了 ____________，胡经理决定打的。

2. 为了让客户 ________，领导指示准时出货。

三、这就……

这 refers to 'right now.' 就 refers to 'immediately.' 这就 indicates that the action of the verb which directly follows will be carried out immediately.

- 我这就通知业务部门。
- 总经理："请通知客户我的出差行程。"
  秘书："我这就跟客户联络。"

1. 客人："服务员，我们点的红烧鱼怎么还没来？"

   服务员："我们这就 ________。"

2. 李："我们去外滩附近看看，怎么样？"

张："好主意，我们这就 ________。"

听力理解 Listening Comprehension (30)

( ) 1. 谁决定请中友公司吃饭的时间？

❶经理 ❷总经理 ❸公司

( ) 2. 下面哪句话是对的？

❶四月三号晚上6点请中友公司吃饭。

❷在北京楼吃饭的预算有问题。

❸在北京楼吃饭费用很高。

( ) 1. 是谁让公司市场更大的？ ❶厂长 ❷总经理 ❸主任

( ) 2. 下面哪句话是对的？

❶主任指示得很正确。 ❷总经理常夸奖厂长。

❸为了跟"三资企业"建立关系，大家合作得很好。

阅读理解 Reading Comprehension

下面是十全公司的产品和价钱，十全公司说如果买50个的话，可以打九折。为了给客户送礼，中友贸易公司的总经理指示孙经理负责采购春节礼品。今年中友贸易公司的预算是4万元，旧客户一共有108个，新客户有19个，如果你是孙经理的话，请问你要怎么采购？请写在下一页的采购表里：

十全食品公司商品表

产品名：年糕
价钱：$ 200
九折价：$ 180

产品名：肉干
价钱：$ 180
九折价：$ 162

产品名：茗茶
价钱：$ 250
九折价：$ 225

产品名：茅台酒
价钱：$ 300
九折价：$ 270

商品数量满50个，可再打九折。欢迎各公司采购！

中友贸易公司春节礼品采购表				
礼品 数量 客户	年糕	( )	肉干	( )
新客户	( )	( )	( )	( )
旧客户	( )	( )	( )	( )
费用：	( )			

你怎么说？ How Would You Say It?

( ) 1. 出货时间得再安排。

( ) 2. 三节一定要送礼吗？

( ) 3. 最近客户下单减少了。

( ) 4. 总经理指示要跟“三资企业”建立关系。

( ) 5. 小吴决定报告领导是正确的。

( ) 6. 业务部门说新客户增加了，

A 是的，这是为了交际的考量。

B 交际应酬的费用一定要提高。

C 可不，要不然我们就麻烦了。

D 是的，请领导指示。

E 这是怎么回事？

F 我这就通知业务部门。

English Translation

Yang: Mr. Hu *(literally: Manager Hu)*, the budget chart shows that the amount of money being used to entertain clients is more than it used to be. What's the deal?

Hu: That's because the business department raised their gift-purchasing budget for the Dragon Boat Festival, Mid-Autumn Festival and Spring Festival.

Yang: In order to make maintaining business relations with our clients go more smoothly, we are going to give gifts for Chinese New Years and other major festivals in addition to wining and dining them. But, with a budget this high, if we raise it in one place, it has to be lowered somewhere else.

Hu: Recently our company has become interested in working together with some foreign-funded enterprises in Shenzhen *(literally: the three types of companies with foreign investment and / or management allowed under Chinese law)*, so the number of companies that we need to give gifts to has increased by more than ten.

Yang: Establishing relationships with new clients is the right thing to do. However, whether it's necessary to raise the gift-purchasing budget is something that still needs to be looked into.

Hu: What do you suggest? *(Literally: Please make a suggestion.)*

Yang: I think we should keep giving gifts to our old customers as before. As far as new customers, we should see how many orders they place and then decide what kind of gift to give them.

Hu: OK. I'll inform the business department.

工商文化智库 Business-Culture Knowledge Trove

- In order to establish long-term stable working relationships with clients, Chinese business people are accustomed to giving gifts to their clients for the three major Chinese holidays. When choosing a gift, it's best to consider the client's preferences. Otherwise, tea or alcohol is also considered appropriate gifts.
- In the Chinese business world, the entertaining of business clients has been considered a necessity since ancient times. From playing Mahjong to golf, from putting on banquets to offering snacks and beverages and the drinking of copious amounts of alcohol are all ways of competing for new orders and creating new business opportunities. These things should not be taken lightly.
- 三资企业 refers to the three types of companies which are funded or operated according to one of the three ways foreign investment and foreign management are allowed in China under Chinese law, namely: 1. Chinese-foreign equity joint ventures, 2. Chinese-foreign contractual joint ventures or 3. wholly foreign-owned enterprises.

1. 中外合资企业 *Chinese-foreign equity joint venture* refers to foreign companies, businesses and other financial institutions or individuals who are approved by the Chinese government, according to the principle of equality and mutual benefit, to engage in business within the borders of the People's Republic of China by investing, managing, incurring risk as well as sharing gains and losses together with Chinese companies, businesses and other financial institutions or individuals.

2. 中外合营企业 The term *Chinese-foreign contractual joint venture* refers to foreign companies, enterprises and other economic organizations or individuals that are allowed to jointly operate a company according to the principle of equality and mutual benefit with enterprises or other economic organizations within the borders of the People's Republic of China in order to expand foreign economic cooperation and technological exchange. These non-equity partners operate according to the various contractual terms and conditions for investment, such as profit distribution, risk liability, mode of operation, etc.

3. 外资企业 *Wholly foreign-owned enterprise* refers to enterprises established within the borders of the People's Republic of China which are wholly funded by foreign companies, enterprises, other economic organizations or individuals. This does not include branches of foreign companies or other economic organizations established overseas, but located within China.

(Source: http://tw.18dao.net/)

Answer Key

主题词汇 Main Vocabulary

A. 交际、应酬、送礼、费用、礼品

B. 预算表、预算、增加、减少、采购、费用

词语练习 Vocabulary Exercises

1. 更　2. 预算　3. 礼品　4. 应酬　5. 费用
6. 决定　7. 采购　8. 增加　9. 研究　10. 正确

重要句型 Sentence Patterns

一、1. 多
　　2. 忙
二、1. 更快到达机场
　　2. 放心下单
三、1. 上菜
　　2. 走

听力理解 Listening Comprehension

一、1. ❷　2. ❸
二、1. ❸　2. ❶

阅读理解 Reading Comprehension

（略）

你怎么说? How Would You Say It?

1. D　2. A　3. E　4. F　5. C　6. B

Note

8

银行

At the Bank

Learning Objectives

Goals: Going to the bank is daily necessity for business people.

The goals for this lesson are to:

1. understand the difference between exchanging foreign cash and foreign checks
2. learn how to open a bank account and the procedures for depositing and withdrawing money
3. know the differences between a debit card and a credit card

经典佳句 Common Phrases

你的意思是○○○。
Nǐ de yìsi shì OOO.

○○○就不受这个限制了。
OOO jiù bú shòu zhèige xiànzhì le.

我研究研究以后再决定。
Wǒ yánjiū yánjiu yǐhòu zài juédìng.

场景对话 Dialogue (31)

史迪夫：请问，你们牌子上的美元汇价跟我兑换的不一样，这是怎么回事？

行　员：您的兑换单请给我看看。噢，您兑换的是支票，我们牌子上的汇价是美元现金的。

史迪夫：你的意思是用现金兑换人民币，比用支票兑换的钱多，对吗？

行　员：对。您需要开个户头把钱存在我们这儿吗？

史迪夫：是的，我想先把一部分的人民币存着，要用的时候，再来取款。

行　员：行，请您先填开户申请表，再填一张红色的存款单，最后和护照一起给我。

史迪夫：对了，我也要申请信用卡，你们的借记卡就是信用卡吗？

行　员：借记卡是你刷卡的时候，得看户头里还有多少钱，不能超过，信用卡就不受这个限制了。

史迪夫：谢谢，我研究研究以后再决定。

Pinyin for Dialogue

Shǐdífū:	Qǐng wèn, nǐmen páizi shang de Měiyuán huìjià gēn wǒ duìhuàn de bù yíyàng, zhè shì zěnme huíshì?
hángyuán:	Nín de duìhuàndān qǐng gěi wǒ kànkan. Òu, nín duìhuàn de shì zhīpiào, wǒmen páizi shang de huìjià shì Měiyuán xiànjīn de.
Shǐdífū:	Nǐ de yìsi shì yòng xiànjīn duìhuàn Rénmínbì, bǐ yòng zhīpiào duìhuàn de qián duō, duì ma?
hángyuán:	Duì. Nín xūyào kāi ge hùtóu bǎ qián cún zài wǒmen zhèr ma?
Shǐdífū:	Shìde, wǒ xiǎng xiān bǎ yíbùfen de Rénmínbì cúnzhe, yào yòng de shíhou, zài lái qǔkuǎn.
hángyuán:	Xíng, qǐng nín xiān tián kāihù shēnqǐngbiǎo, zài tián yì zhāng hóngsè de cúnkuǎndān, zuìhòu hé hùzhào yìqǐ gěi wǒ.
Shǐdífū:	Duìle, wǒ yě yào shēnqǐng xìnyòngkǎ, nǐmen de jièjìkǎ jiùshì xìnyòngkǎ ma?
hángyuán:	Jièjìkǎ shì nǐ shuākǎ de shíhou, děi kàn hùtóu li háiyǒu duōshao qián, bù néng chāoguò, xìnyòngkǎ jiù bú shòu zhèige xiànzhì le.
Shǐdífū:	Xièxie, wǒ yánjiū yánjiu yǐhòu zài juédìng.

词语 Vocabulary (32)

Learn the Chinese characters and their pronunciations, then complete the writing assignment below.

牌子	*N*	páizi	sign (in front of a store)
汇价	*N*	huìjià	exchange rate
兑换	*V*	duìhuàn	to exchange money
行员	*N*	hángyuán	(bank) teller
单	*N*	dān	piece of paper (as in a receipt, etc.)
支票	*N*	zhīpiào	(bank) check
现金	*N*	xiànjīn	cash
开	*V*	kāi	to open
户头 / 账户	*N*	hùtóu / zhànghù	(bank) account
把	*CV*	bǎ	grammatical word used to place the object before the verb
存	*V*	cún	to store, to deposit; to exist
取款	*VO*	qǔ//kuǎn	to withdraw (money)
填	*V*	tián	to fill out (a form)
存款	*VO*	cún//kuǎn	to deposit (money)
护照	*N*	hùzhào	passport
申请	*V*	shēnqǐng	to apply

借记卡	*N*	jièjìkǎ	debit card
刷卡	*VO*	shuā//kǎ	to use a credit card or debit card *(literally: to swipe a card)*
超过	*V*	chāoguò	to go over, to exceed
受	*V*	shòu	to receive
限制	*N*	xiànzhì	limit; limitation

主题词汇 Main Vocabulary

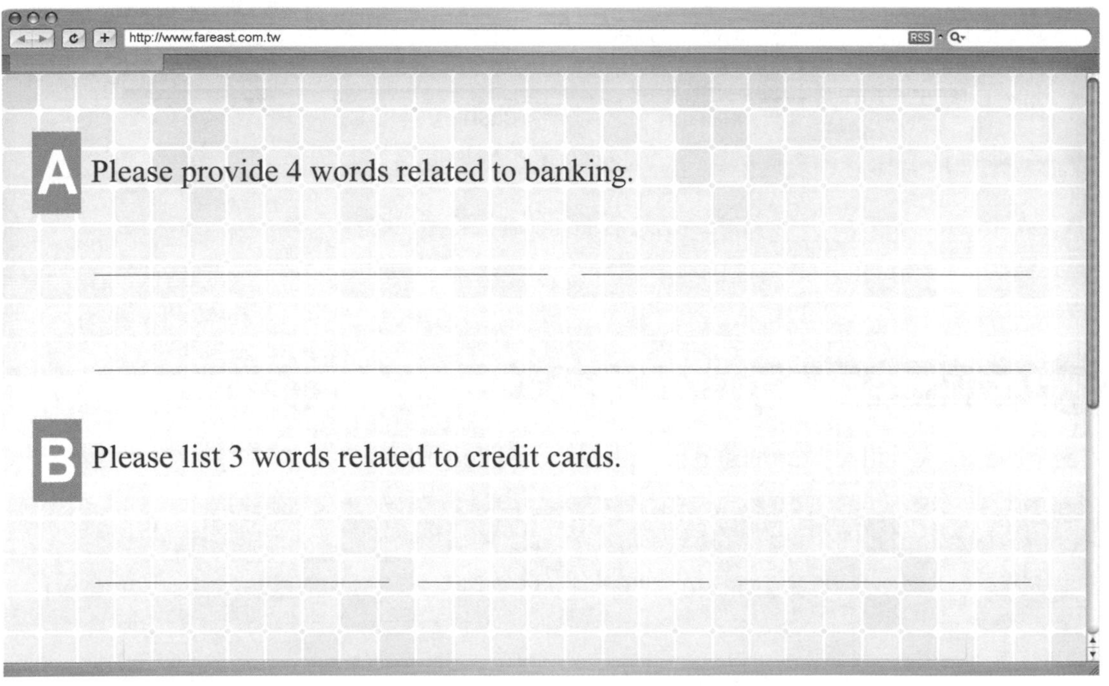

A Please provide 4 words related to banking.

B Please list 3 words related to credit cards.

词语练习 Vocabulary Exercises

Use the words below to fill in the blanks.

现金　户头　申请　把　刷卡　超过　汇价　存　限制　护照

1. 你是外国人，要到酒店外面去最好把 ________ 带着。
2. 对不起，我们这儿不用支票，请您付 ________。
3. 你没填开户申请表，银行怎么给你 ________ 呢？
4. 请问，今天美元的 ________ 是多少？
5. 有些地方打的也可以 ________，非常方便。
6. 采购礼品的费用已经 ________ 预算了。
7. 如果你每天 ________ 钱的话，你的钱就增加了。
8. 带行李上飞机得受一些 ________。
9. 在我们这儿，________ 网络不但快也不麻烦。
10. 秘书 ________ 行程表放在经理的桌子上。

专有名词 Specialized Terms（33）

Learn these specialized terms and complete the related exercises.

Terms	Pinyin	English
史迪夫	Shǐdífū	Steve (transliteration)

实用名词 Practical Vocabulary (33)

Learn the practical vocabulary and complete the related exercises.

Terms	Pinyin	English
美元	Měiyuán	U.S. Dollar
人民币	Rénmínbì	Renminbi (aka Chinese Yuan)
欧元	Ōuyuán	Euro
英镑	Yīngbàng	British Pound
日币	Rìbì	Japanese Yen
开户申请表	kāihù shēnqǐngbiǎo	application for opening an account

重要句型 Sentence Patterns

一、（S）把 O V 在 PW

This sentence pattern emphasizes that S is dealing with O and the result of the action is related to PW.

- 您需要开个户头把钱存在我们这儿吗？
- 请把我的房间安排在安全门附近。

1. 请您把名字 ________ 在这里。

2. 入住的时间还没到，客人可以先把 ________ 放在前台。

二、S 把 O V 着

This sentence pattern emphasizes that S is dealing with O and that the action of V is being maintained.

- 我想先把一部分的人民币存着。

● 出差的时候，你应该把客户的名片带着。

1. 为了买东西方便，小李把 ________ ________ 着。

2. 陈经理现在很忙，所以先把 ________ ________ 着，想不忙的时候再看。

三、S（不）受……限制

This pattern means that S is (not) limited by....

● 信用卡就不受这个限制了。

● 出货时间受生产时间限制。

1. 过年过节送礼受 ________ 限制，不能增加。

2. 上网订房不受 ________ 限制，什么时间，什么地方都能订。

听力理解 Listening Comprehension（34）

( ) 1. 中国人都能在这儿开户吗？

❶是的

❷大人行，小孩儿得受一些限制

❸大人没问题，至于小孩儿，银行要研究研究

( ) 2. 外国人都能在这儿开户吗？

❶不是，没有护照的大人不能开户

❷大人行，小孩得受一些限制

❸大人没问题，至于小孩儿，银行要研究研究

（　）1. 男的为什么不能刷卡？

❶采购礼品的费用不少

❷存款超过刷卡的费用

❸刷卡的费用超过存款

（　）2. 女的说男的应该怎么做？

❶付现金，不要刷这种借记卡

❷存款不够，不能刷这种借记卡

❸先把钱存在户头里再刷卡

阅读理解 Reading Comprehension

Below there are two banking forms. One of them is deposit slip from the Bank of Business. The other one is a debit card application form from Business Banking Corp. Please fill them out.

（一）、存款单

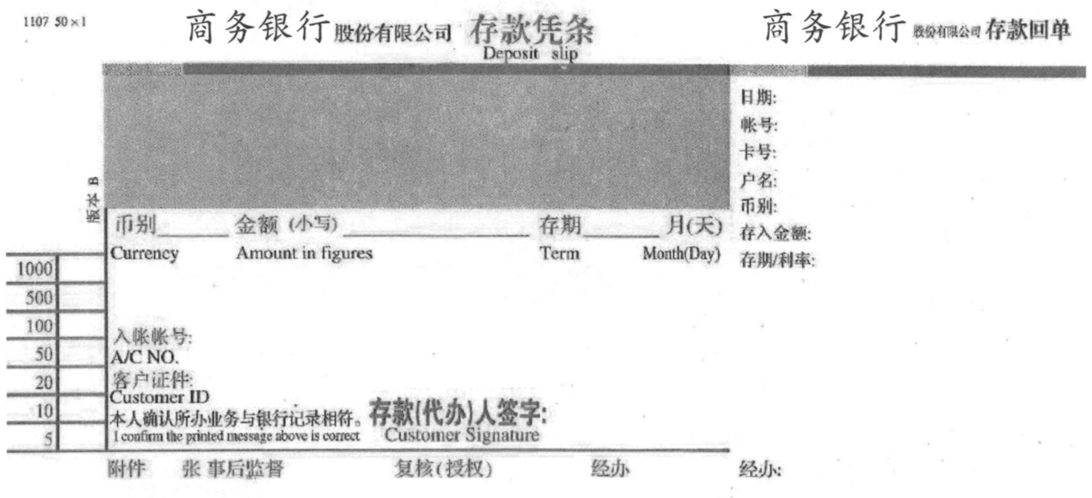

1107 50×1

商务银行股份有限公司 存款凭条 Deposit slip

商务银行股份有限公司存款回单

版本 B

币别____ 金额（小写）____ 存期____ 月(天)
Currency Amount in figures Term Month(Day)

1000
500
100
50
20
10
5

入帐帐号:
A/C NO.
客户证件:
Customer ID
本人确认所办业务与银行记录相符。 存款(代办)人签字:
I confirm the printed message above is correct Customer Signature

附件 张 事后监督 复核(授权) 经办

日期:
帐号:
卡号:
户名:
币别:
存入金额:
存期/利率:
经办:

（二）、借记卡申请表

流水号

商务银联借记卡申请表

申请业务类型 □开卡 □变更客户信息　　申请卡级别 □主卡 □附属卡

客户基本信息项1（必填） 1

姓名　　性别 □男 □女　　国籍

证件种类 □居民身份证（含临时） □户口簿 □军官证 □警官证 □士兵证 □军事院校学员证 □军官退休证 □文职干部证 □文职干部退休证 □港澳居民往来内地通行证 □台湾居民来往大陆通行证 □外国公民护照 □其他（请注明）________

证件号码

有效期限 ____________ 至 ____________

发证机关 ________________________

客户基本信息项2（新客户必填，必填项若无可填内容，填"无"） 2

拼音或英文姓名

出生日期　　年　　月　　日

住所地址或联系地址

邮政编码

家庭电话　　手机

职　　业 □行政管理 □金融 □航空运输 □邮电通讯 □律师 □会计师 □信息产业 □能源产业 □娱乐服务业 □餐饮业 □建筑业 □旅游业 □社会服务业 □农业渔牧业 □采掘业 □制造业 □保险业 □销售 □其他（请注明）________

紧急联系人（不承担担保责任）：

姓　　名

家庭电话　　手机

客户其他信息项（首次申请贵宾卡必填，其他可选） 3

工作单位

办公电话

E-mail

职　　务 □一般职员 □部门经理 □总经理 □一般干部 □科级 □处级 □厅局级及以上 □其他（请注明）________

月收入（元） □1000以下 □1000－2000 □2000－3000 □3000－5000 □5000－8000 □8000－10000 □10000－20000 □20000以上

房产性质 □无住房 □自购商品房 □自购公有住房 □家属所有房 □其他（请注明）________

婚姻状况 □已婚 □未婚 □其他（请注明）________

教育程度 □博士及以上 □硕士 □本科 □大专 □中专／高中 □初中及以下

兴趣爱好（可多项） □运动健身 □休闲购物 □文学赏析 □收藏品鉴赏 □旅游 □投资理财 □艺术音乐 □饮食文化 □插花技巧 □烹调技术 □色彩搭配 □形象设计 □其他________

开户银行代码

申请主卡信息项 4

申请卡种 □普通卡 □金卡 □钻石卡 □其他卡（请注明）________

预选卡号（金卡、钻石卡可选）

注：请在方框内顺序填写您选择的卡号中的7位数字（第一位只能填数字0－4），如不填写，系统将自动生成卡号。

以下内容仅在委托他人申请主卡时填写

代理人姓名　　代理人证件类型

代理人证件号码

申请附属卡的主持卡人信息项 5

姓名　　证件类型

证件号码

主卡卡号（申请附属卡填写）

申请附属卡等级 □A级 □B级 □C级

签名项 6

兹申明：

1、以上填写内容完全属实。

2、本人已收到并仔细阅读了《民生银联借记卡用卡规定》的全部内容，自愿签署并遵守各项规定。

申请人本人或代理人签名

年　　月　　日

贵宾卡审批项 7

审批部门签章：　　审批人签章：

年　　月　　日

银行专用项 8

卡　　号

开户银行名称

银行盖章：

经办（签章）：

复核（签章）：

推荐人（员工号）

第一联　开户银行作开户资料留存

你怎么说？How Would You Say It?

( ) 1. 牌子上的汇价是美元现金的，

( ) 2. 我想存款，应该怎么办？

( ) 3. 你要申请什么卡？

( ) 4. 请问，3千元人民币可以兑换多少美元？

( ) 5. 你刷的是信用卡还是借记卡？

( ) 6. 刷借记卡得受存款限制。

A 你要先开户才行。

B 得看汇价，每天都不一样。

C 你的意思是不是我得先把钱存在户头里？

D 比美元支票高一点儿。

E 两种不是都一样吗？

F 我研究研究以后再决定。

English Translation

Steve: Excuse me, the exchange rate on your sign for American dollars is different from the rate I got. Why is that?

teller: May I see your exchange receipt? Oh, you exchanged a check. The rate on the sign is for cash.

Steve: You mean that I'd get more money for exchanging cash into Renminbi than for a check? Is that right?

teller: Right. Would you like to open an account with us and deposit your money here?

Steve: Yes. I would like to deposit some of the money and then come back and withdraw it when I need it.

teller: OK. Please first fill out an application for opening an account, then fill out a red deposit slip. Lastly, give those to me together with your passport.

Steve: Oh, yeah. I also want to apply for a credit card. Isn't the credit card the same as a debit card?

teller: When using the debit card, you need to see how much money you have in your account. You can't exceed that amount. The credit card doesn't have this limitation.

Steve: Thanks. I'll look into this and then make a decision.

工商文化智库 Business-Culture Knowledge Trove

- Traditionally, Chinese people are not very accepting of the practice of overdrawing. The first bank established without the help of foreign capital wasn't founded until 1897. Before that, people were used to keeping money on their person and weren't even comfortable with leaving their money in old-style private Chinese banks. Money was only borrowed when there were no other alternatives and was considered shameful. If it truly became necessary, it was a favor to be asked of friends or family.
- At the beginning of the 20th century, under the influence of the West, people began putting their money in banks. In spite of this, very few people, other than business people, borrowed from banks. It wasn't until the 21st century that a portion of the population began to have the idea of borrowing money in order to establish personal credit.

Answer Key

主题词汇 Main Vocabulary

A. 汇价、存款、取款、户头、兑换、支票

B. 申请、超过、借记卡、刷卡、信用卡

词语练习 Vocabulary Exercises

1. 护照 2. 现金 3. 户头 4. 汇价 5. 刷卡

6. 超过 7. 存 8. 限制 9. 申请 10. 把

重要句型 Sentence Patterns

一、1. 填

2. 行李

二、1. 信用卡；带

2. 资料；放

三、1. 公司预算

2. 时间和地方

听力理解 Listening Comprehension

一、1. ❷ 2. ❶

二、1. ❸ 2. ❸

阅读理解 Reading Comprehension

（略）

你怎么说？ How Would You Say It?

1. D 2. A 3. F 4. B 5. E 6. C

Note

9 介绍产品
Demonstrating a New Product

Learning Objectives

When selling merchandise, the way a product is introduced to a potential customer is crucial. In this lesson, the student will learn how to introduce a product's:

1. styles and functions
2. size and colors
3. market price

经典佳句 Common Phrases

欢迎参观我们的展示室。这是下一季要推出的手机。外型和功能都是最新的。
Huānyíng cānguān wǒmen de zhǎnshìshì. Zhè shì xià yí jì yào tuīchū de shǒujī. Wàixíng hé gōngnéng dōu shì zuì xīn de.

外型又小又薄，看起来很时尚。
Wàixíng yòu xiǎo yòu báo, kàn qilai hěn shíshàng.

这样的手机，市场的反应一定不错，价钱一定不便宜。
Zhèyàng de shǒujī, shìchǎng de fǎnyìng yídìng búcuò, jiàqián yídìng bù piányi.

场景对话 Dialogue (35)

王：李经理，欢迎参观我们的展示室。这是下一季要推出的手机。外型和功能都是最新的。

李：贵公司生产的手机，外型又小又薄，看起来很时尚，不知道功能怎么样？

王：这型手机，除了打电话的功能，还可以照相、录影、上网、玩游戏和看电影。

李：现在的手机，功能越来越多，差不多跟小型电脑一样。有什么颜色？

王：颜色有银色的、黑色的和红色的，都是最新流行的，也是最受年轻人欢迎的。

李：真漂亮，尺寸很小，差不多只有两吋，重不重？我可以拿拿看吗？

王：没问题，我们的产品不但外型美，功能多，拿起来也很轻。

李：真的很轻。这样的手机，市场的反应一定不错。价钱一定不便宜。

X167 折叠式手机

- 2.2吋彩色萤幕
- 超大铃声，超大字体
- SOS紧急求救键
- FM收音机
- 汉语拼音输入

（颜色：银、红、黑）

$3,388

Pinyin for Dialogue

Wáng: Lǐ jīnglǐ, huānyíng cānguān wǒmen de zhǎnshìshì. Zhè shì xià yí jì yào tuīchū de shǒujī. Wàixíng hé gōngnéng dōu shì zuì xīn de.

Lǐ: Guì gōngsī shēngchǎn de shǒujī, wàixíng yòu xiǎo yòu báo, kàn qilai hěn shíshàng, bù zhīdao gōngnéng zěnmeyàng?

Wáng: Zhèi xíng shǒujī, chúle dǎ diànhuà de gōngnéng, hái kěyǐ zhàoxiàng, lùyǐng, shàngwǎng, wán yóuxì hé kàn diànyǐng.

Lǐ: Xiànzài de shǒujī, gōngnéng yuè lai yuè duō, chàbuduō gēn xiǎo xíng diànnǎo yíyàng. Yǒu shénme yánsè?

Wáng: Yánsè yǒu yínsè de, hēisè de hé hóngsè de, dōu shì zuì xīn liúxíng de, yě shì zuì shòu niánqīngrén huānyíng de.

Lǐ: Zhēn piàoliang, chǐcùn hěn xiǎo, chàbuduō zhǐyǒu liǎng cùn, zhòng bú zhòng? Wǒ kěyǐ nána kàn ma?

Wáng: Méi wèntí, wǒmen de chǎnpǐn búdàn wàixíng měi, gōngnéng duō, ná qilai yě hěn qīng.

Lǐ: Zhēnde hěn qīng. Zhèyàng de shǒujī, shìchǎng de fǎnyìng yídìng búcuò. Jiàqián yídìng bù piányi.

(36)

Learn the Chinese characters and their pronunciations, then complete the writing assignment below.

参观	*V*	cānguān	to visit
展示室	*N*	zhǎnshìshì	showroom
季	*N*	jì	season (of the year)

推出	*V*	tuīchū	to release to the public (said of products, books, etc.)
手机	*N*	shǒujī	mobile phone; cellphone
外型	*N*	wàixíng	(external) appearance
功能	*N*	gōngnéng	function
薄	*SV*	báo	thin (said of things)
时尚	*SV*	shíshàng	stylish
录影	*VO*	lùyǐng	to record video
玩游戏	*VO*	wán//yóuxì	to play games
越来越	*PT*	yuè lai yuè	more and more
型	*N*	xíng	model; type
银色	*N*	yínsè	the color light gray
黑色	*N*	hēisè	the color black
流行	*SV*	liúxíng	popular
年轻人	*N*	niánqīngrén	young people
尺寸	*N*	chǐcùn	size; measurement
吋	*M/N*	cùn	(English) inch
重	*SV*	zhòng	heavy
轻	*SV*	qīng	light
支	*M*	zhī	measure word for mobile phones; branch, twig

主题词汇 Main Vocabulary

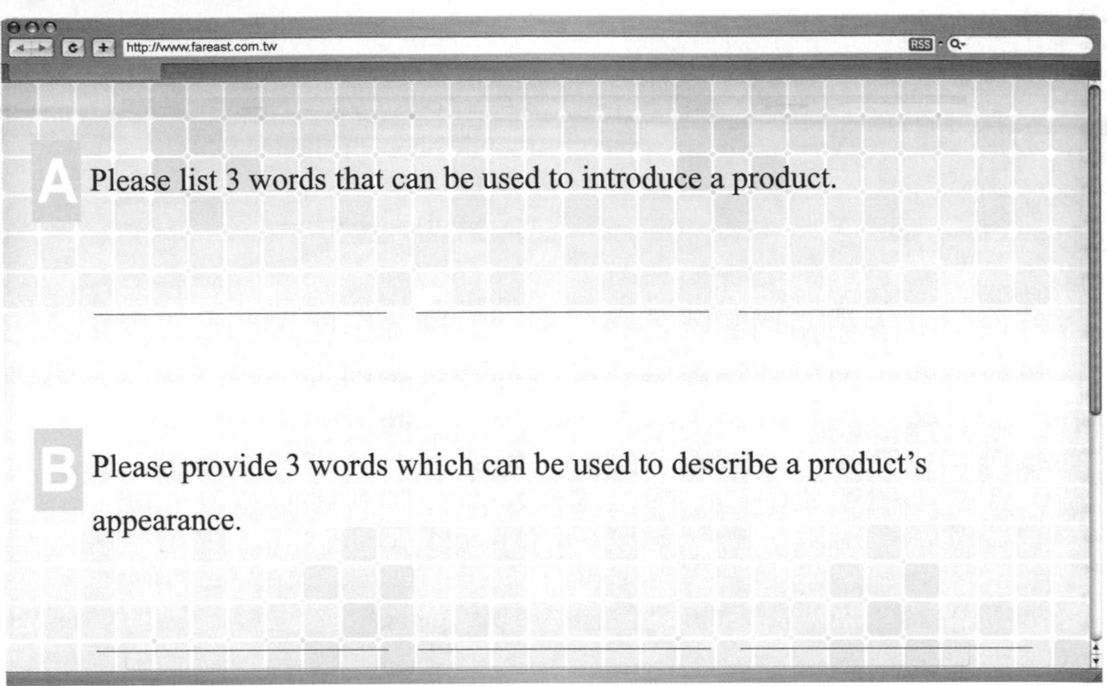

A Please list 3 words that can be used to introduce a product.

______________ ______________ ______________

B Please provide 3 words which can be used to describe a product's appearance.

______________ ______________ ______________

词语练习 Vocabulary Exercises

Use the words below to fill in the blanks.

展示室　推出　外型　功能　时尚　录影　流行　尺寸　吋　重　轻

1. 这支手机的 ____________ 很多，可以照相，也可以玩游戏。
2. 今年 ____________ 的银色，最受年轻人欢迎。
3. 手机的 ____________ 看起来很时尚，拿起来很轻。
4. 外型 ____________ 的产品都很受年轻人喜欢。
5. 数码相机的 ____________ 做得一年比一年小。
6. 请问贵公司下一季要 ____________ 什么新产品？

7. 这个大型的电视，有几 __________？

8. 这个数码相机很小，可是拿起来很 __________。

9. A：欢迎参观我们的 __________，里面有很多新产品。

B：谢谢。又新又大，产品真不少。

10. 手机越来越薄，拿起来也越来越 __________。

实用名词 Practical Vocabulary (37)

Learn the practical vocabulary and complete the related exercises.

Terms	Pinyin	English
智慧型手机	zhìhuìxíng shǒujī	smart phone
笔记型电脑（笔电）	bǐjìxíng diànnǎo (bǐdiàn)	notebook (computer)
数码相机	shùmǎ xiàngjī	digital camera

重要句型 Sentence Patterns

一、……又……又……

又 expresses accumulation of the states or conditions which precede and follow it.

- 贵公司生产的手机，外型又小又薄。
- 笔记型电脑拿起来又轻又时尚。

1. 数码相机又 __________ 又 __________。

2. 贵公司的产品又 __________ 又 __________。

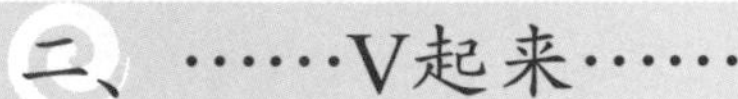

二、……V起来……

When V起来 followed by an adjective, it expresses an appraisal or perception of some aspect of the thing or object which precedes it.

- 外型又小又薄，看起来很时尚。
- 我们的产品功能多，拿起来也很轻。

1. 这间展示室看起来很 ________。

2. 这个笔记型电脑的颜色看起来很 ________，
   可是拿起来很 ________。

三、越来越……

越来越…… expresses that the extent or degree of the adjective which follows it increases with time. It can only have one subject.

- 现在的手机，功能越来越多。
- 电脑的颜色越来越漂亮。

1. 市场的反应越来越 ________。

2. 数码相机的价钱越来越 ________。

四、VV看

In colloquial speech, VV看 means to try performing the action of the verb (V). Only single syllable verbs can be used in this construction.

- 我可以拿拿看吗？
- 红烧鱼很好吃，你要不要吃吃看？

1. 这个 ________ 不错，你要不要玩玩看？

2. 那枝笔很好，你可以 ________ 看。

听力理解 Listening Comprehension (38)

( ) 1. 这些智慧型手机

❶下个月要推出 ❷下一季要推出 ❸下个周末要推出

( ) 2. 智慧型手机

❶只有打电话的功能

❷什么功能都有，但是不能看电影

❸一共有6个功能

( ) 1. 智慧型手机的功能

❶差不多像小型电脑一样

❷比小型电脑多一点

❸功能跟小型电脑不一样，但是颜色比小型电脑多

( ) 2. 智慧型手机的颜色

❶只有银色、黑色和红色

❷什么颜色都受年轻人欢迎

❸只有银色、黑色和红色最受年轻人欢迎的

Below is a list of products from the Yangyang Science and Technology Company. Please fill out the table based upon the information provided in the audio.

产品	颜色	尺寸	外型	价钱
笔记型____	银色	________吋	又轻又好看	美金____元
新型______	__________	________吋	又____又____	美金1,200元
__________	黑色	________吋	____________	美金3,350元

阅读理解 Reading Comprehension

李明全是十全科技公司采购部的主任，他上个月去广州参观洋洋科技公司的展示室。那间展示室又新又大，里面的产品都是下一季要推出的，有手机、数码相机和电视。外型看起来都又漂亮又时尚，功能也不少。至于颜色，只有银色、黑色和红色，颜色不多，但都是最受年轻人欢迎的。

展示室里的手机和数码相机，尺寸都很小，拿起来也很轻。平常带着很方便；至于电视机，都是现在新流行的大型电视。李主任想这些产品市场的反应一定不错，很想马上下单，但是他得跟总经理研究以后再决定。

( ) 1. 展示室里面的产品

❶都是大型的

❷都是小型的

❸有大型的，也有小型的

( ) 2. 李主任去广州参观洋洋公司的展示室以后，最后他

❶马上下单

❷跟总经理研究以后再决定下单的事

❸决定不要下单

( ) 3. 洋洋公司的产品

❶颜色很多，都是最受年轻人欢迎的

❷只有三个颜色

❸只有银色、黑色和红色那三个颜色不受年轻人欢迎

你怎么说？ How Would You Say It?

(　)	1. 智慧型手机有什么功能？	A	看起来不大，拿起来很轻。
(　)	2. 这个数码相机重不重？	B	带着不方便。
(　)	3. 什么颜色的手机最好卖？	C	外型又小又薄，看起来很时尚的。
(　)	4. 十全公司推出的智慧型手机，	D	除了打电话，还可以照相、录影、上网、玩游戏和看电影。
(　)	5. 大型的相机不好吗？	E	市场的反应好，价钱不便宜。
(　)	6. 什么样的手机最受年轻人欢迎？	F	受年轻人欢迎的颜色都好卖。

English Translation

Ms. Wang: Mr. Li *(literally: Manager Li)*, welcome to our showroom. These are the mobile phones which are going to be released next season. Their forms and functions are both the very newest design.

Mr. Li: The phones produced by your company are both small and thin. They look very fashionable. What about their functionality?

Ms. Wang: This model here, in addition to its function as a phone, can take pictures, record video and access the Internet. It also provides games and movies.

Mr. Li: These days, mobile phones are getting more and more functionality. They are almost like little computers. What colors are available?

Ms. Wang: Recently, light gray, black and red are the most popular and liked the most by young people.

Mr. Li: Very nice *(literally: very pretty)*. They are fairly small, only about 2 inches in length. Are they heavy? Can I hold one?

Ms. Wang: No problem. Besides having an attractive form and a lot of functionality, they are also light in weight.

Mr. Li: It is really light. This type of phone will definitely have a good market reaction and it certainly won't be cheap.

工商文化智库 Business-Culture Knowledge

- There are many types of electronics. Among them, computers, digital cameras and mobile phones are things almost everyone needs. New styles, functions, colors and sizes come out each day. New products are continuously replacing the old ones as prices get cheaper and cheaper. Consumers, especially the younger ones, are not fainthearted about their spending money as long as it looks fashionable and has a lot of functionality.
- All-in-one computers, e-books and 4D televisions are currently the most fashionable and are brimming with business opportunities.

主题词汇 Main Vocabulary

A. 外型、功能、尺寸、颜色

B. 小、薄、时尚

词语练习 Vocabulary Exercises

1. 功能　2. 流行　3. 外型　4. 时尚　5. 尺寸
6. 推出　7. 吋　8. 重　9. 展示室　10. 轻

重要句型 Sentence Patterns

一、1. 小；轻
　　2. 便宜；时尚

二、1. 新
　　2. 漂亮；重

三、1. 好
　　2. 便宜

四、1. 游戏
　　2. 写写

听力理解 Listening Comprehension

一、1. ❷　2. ❸

二、1. ❶　2. ❸

三、

产品	颜色	尺寸	外型	价钱
笔记型电脑		十八吋		美金1,999元
新型手机	红色	两吋	又小又薄	
大型电视		六十五吋	时尚	

阅读理解 Reading Comprehension

1. ❸ 2. ❷ 3. ❷

你怎么说? How Would You Say It?

1. D 2. A 3. F 4. E 5. B 6. C

Note

10

参观展览
Attending an Electronics Exhibition

Learning Objectives

New products enter the market every day. Business people can learn about these products by attending exhibitions. In this lesson, using the attending of an exhibition as the main theme, you will learn to introduce:

1. an exhibition's theme and its products
2. the companies participating in the exhibition and their booths
3. the exhibition's opening times and purpose

经典佳句 Common Phrases

我去参观消费电子展览。昨天一结束，我就回来了。

Wǒ qù cānguān xiāofèi diànzǐ zhǎnlǎn. Zuótiān yì jiéshù, wǒ jiù huílai le.

虽然新产品很多，不过，我觉得最特别的是电子书、立体电视和云端科技产品。

Suīrán xīn chǎnpǐn hěn duō, búguò, wǒ juéde zuì tèbié de shì diànzǐ shū, lìtǐ diànshì hé yúnduān kējì chǎnpǐn.

前四天是专业贸易时间，只让有邀请卡的买家或贸易商参观，至于一般人在后两天才能进去。

Qián sì tiān shì zhuānyè màoyì shíjiān, zhǐ ràng yǒu yāoqǐng kǎ de mǎijiā huò màoyìshāng cānguān, zhìyú yìbān rén zài hòu liǎng tiān cái néng jìnqù.

场景对话 Dialogue (39)

王：听说你上个星期到香港去参观电子展览了。

李：是，我去参观消费电子展览。昨天一结束，我就回来了。

王：这次有多少厂商参加展览？

李：一共有六百多家，包括美洲、欧洲和亚洲的厂商，差不多有两千个摊位。

王：这么大型的展览，有特别的新产品吗？

李：有。虽然新产品很多，不过，我觉得最特别的是电子书、立体电视和云端科技产品。

王：科技进步得真快，高科技产品越来越多。这次展览一共几天？谁都可以进去参观吗？

李：一共六天。前四天是专业贸易时间，只让有邀请卡的买家或贸易商参观，至于一般人在后两天才能进去。

王：会场里面参观的人这么多，工作人员都很忙吧？

李：对，工作人员都忙着介绍他们的新产品。各国的买家、贸易商在一起，有的谈以后的合作，有的直接下单。

Pinyin for Dialogue

Wáng:	Tīngshuō nǐ shàng ge xīngqī dào Xiānggǎng qù cānguān diànzǐ zhǎnlǎn le.
Lǐ:	Shì, wǒ qù cānguān xiāofèi diànzǐ zhǎnlǎn. Zuótiān yì jiéshù, wǒ jiù huílai le.
Wáng:	Zhèi cì yǒu duōshao chǎngshāng cānjiā zhǎnlǎn?
Lǐ:	Yígòng yǒu liù bǎi duō jiā, bāokuò Měizhōu, Ōuzhōu hé Yàzhōu de chǎngshāng, chàbuduō yǒu liǎng qiān ge tānwèi.
Wáng:	Zhème dàxíng de zhǎnlǎn, yǒu tèbié de xīn chǎnpǐn ma?
Lǐ:	Yǒu. Suīrán xīn chǎnpǐn hěn duō, búguò, wǒ juéde zuì tèbié de shì diànzǐ shū, lìtǐ diànshì hé yúnduān kējì chǎnpǐn.
Wáng:	Kējì jìnbù de zhēn kuài, gāo kējì chǎnpǐn yuè lai yuè duō. Zhèi cì zhǎnlǎn yígòng jǐ tiān? Shéi dōu kěyǐ jìnqù cānguān ma?
Lǐ:	Yígòng liù tiān. Qián sì tiān shì zhuānyè màoyì shíjiān, zhǐ ràng yǒu yāoqǐngkǎ de mǎijiā huò màoyìshāng cānguān, zhìyú yìbān rén zài hòu liǎng tiān cái néng jìnqù.
Wáng:	Huìchǎng lǐmiàn cānguān de rén zhème duō, gōngzuò rényuán dōu hěn máng ba?
Lǐ:	Duì, gōngzuò rényuán dōu mángzhe jièshào tāmen de xīn chǎnpǐn. Gè guó de mǎijiā, màoyìshāng zài yìqǐ, yǒude tán yǐhòu de hézuò, yǒude zhíjiē xiàdān.

词语 Vocabulary (40)

Learn the Chinese characters and their pronunciations, then complete the writing assignment below.

展览	*N*	zhǎnlǎn	exhibition; display
电子	*N*	diànzǐ	electronic; an electron
结束	*V*	jiéshù	to conclude; to end
次	*M*	cì	time (as in "this time")
厂商	*N*	chǎngshāng	business; firm; manufacturer
参加	*V*	cānjiā	to attend
摊位	*N*	tānwèi	exhibition booth
特别	*SV*	tèbié	special; unusual
虽然	*Conj*	suīrán	despite; in spite of; although
进步	*V*	jìnbù	to advance, to make progress
专业	*SV*	zhuānyè	professional; specialized
贸易	*N*	màoyì	trade; business
邀请卡	*N*	yāoqǐngkǎ	invitation card
买家	*N*	mǎijiā	buyer (for a company)
或	*Conj*	huò	or
贸易商	*N*	màoyìshāng	trader (also importer / exporter)
一般人	*N*	yìbān rén	normal people; the average person
会场	*N*	huìchǎng	meeting place
人员	*N*	rényuán	personnel
直接	*Adv*	zhíjiē	directly

主题词汇 Main Vocabulary

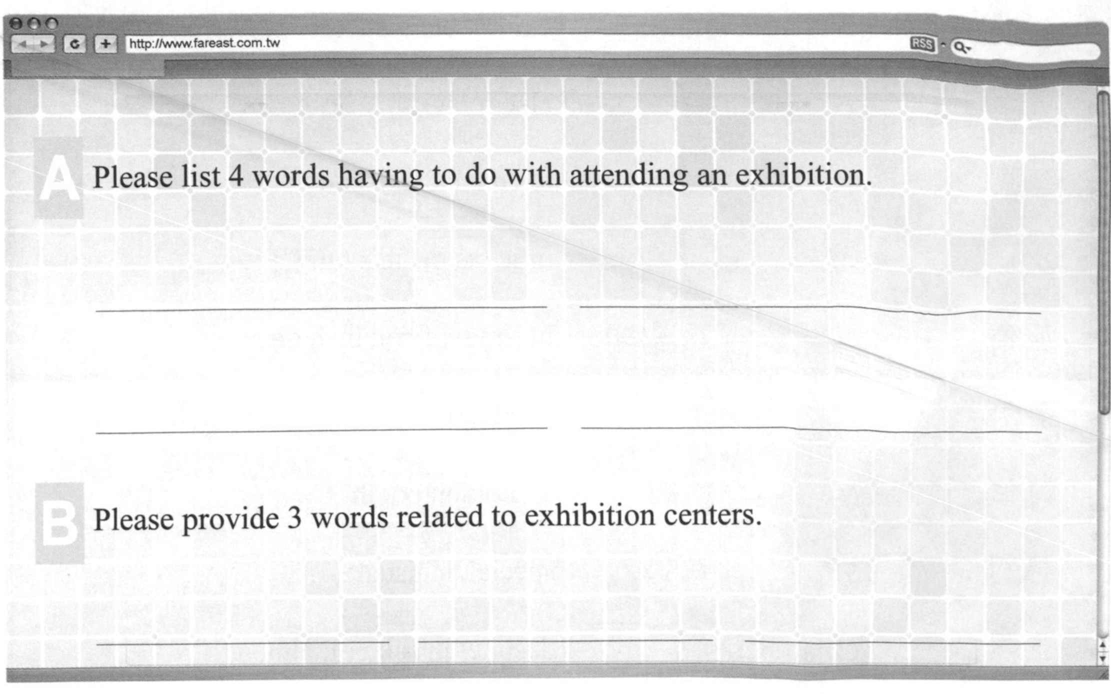

词语练习 Vocabulary Exercises

Use the words below to fill in the blanks.

结束　厂商　特别　虽然　次　专业　一般人　才　会场　人员　下单

1. 贸易商或 ________ 都可以参观商展。
2. 在 ________ 里，买家看到喜欢的产品就可以直接下单。
3. 今年参加展览的 ________ ，一共有一千多家。
4. 今天只让贸易商参观，一般人明天 ________ 可以参观。
5. 这几天是 ________ 贸易时间，一般人不可以进去。
6. 这 ________ 展览的摊位虽然很多，不过参观的人很少。

7. 消费电子展览是什么时候 __________ 的？

8. 工作 __________ 忙着介绍电子书和立体电视。

9. 智慧型手机是展览中最 __________ 的新产品。

10. 买家要是喜欢的话，可以直接 __________。

专有名词 Specialized Terms (41)

Learn these specialized terms and complete the related exercises.

Terms	Pinyin	English
香港	Xiānggǎng	Hong Kong
美洲	Měizhōu	the Americas
欧洲	Ōuzhōu	Europe
亚洲	Yàzhōu	Asia

实用名词 Practical Vocabulary (41)

Learn the practical vocabulary and complete the related exercises.

Terms	Pinyin	English
消费电子展览	xiāofèi diànzǐ zhǎnlǎn	consumer electronics exhibition
电子书	diànzǐ shū	e-book
立体电视	lìtǐ diànshì	4D television
云端科技产品	yúnduān kējì chǎnpǐn	cloud computing technology products

重要句型 Sentence Patterns

一、虽然……，不过……

虽然 is a conjunction that indicates a transition and means that even though condition A is accepted as true, it does not mean that condition B must be rejected. The first clause can either precede or follow the subject. The second clause may used in conjunction with 但是/可是/还是/仍然/不过, etc.

- 虽然新产品很多，不过，我觉得最特别的是电子书、立体电视和云端科技产品。
- 存款虽然不够，不过可以刷卡。

1. 虽然参展的厂商很多，不过 __________ 很少。
2. 我虽然有他的名片，不过我们不常 ________。

二、让

让 means either "*to result in*" or "*to allow, tolerate.*" This sentence pattern is followed by a pivot. The pattern is S + 让 + O + V. For this pattern, the O is also the S for the following V.

- 前四天是专业贸易时间，只让有邀请卡的买家或贸易商参观。
- 这件事，让我研究研究再决定。

1. 父母不让孩子玩太多电脑 ________。
2. 机场的工作人员，不让没有 ________ 的人入关。

三、……才……

才 is an adverb and indicates that only under circumstances, or only for a given reason or purpose, will the conditions following 才 occur or be met. It often works in conjunction with 只有, 必须, 要不, 因为, 由于, 为了 from the preceding clause.

● 一般人在后两天才能进去。

● 年轻人觉得只有买智慧型手机才叫时尚。

1. 这些产品，因为原料涨价了，我们才 ________。

2. 有 ________ 的外国人，才可以在这家银行开户。

四、吧

When used at the end of an interrogative statement, the statement is usually not merely posing a question, but carries the tone of conjecture. If one of the adverbs 也许 or 大概 appears in a sentence, then the sentence cannot end in 吗, only in 吧.

● 工作人员都很忙吧?

● 电子书、立体电视和云端科技产品都是最新的高科技产品吧?

1. 智慧型手机有很多 ________ 吧?

2. 这次消费电子展览参加的 ________，一定不少吧?

 听力理解 Listening Comprehension (42)

1

( ) 1. 那位先生什么时候可以参观?

❶今天 ❷明天 ❸什么时候都可以

( ) 2. 专业贸易时间有什么限制?

❶不让买家或贸易商参观

❷明天才可以参观

❸有邀请卡的人才能参观

(　)1. 消费电子展览

❶今年参加展览的厂商和摊位比去年多

❷去年参加展览的厂商和摊位比今年多

❸今年参加展览的厂商和摊位跟去年一样多

(　)2. 今年消费电子展览的高科技产品

❶各国买家和贸易商都觉得很特别

❷各国买家和贸易商都没有喜欢的

❸各国买家和贸易商都很喜欢

The table below is for the Spring Business Convention in Beijing. Please fill in your answers based upon the information given in the audio.

展览内容	展览时间
春季________展览	三月八日到______月______日
食品展览	____月____日到____月____日
________展览	____月____日到____月____日
消费电子展览	____月____日到五月三十一日

阅读理解 Reading Comprehension

李总经理代表中天科技公司去香港参观消费电子展览，这次有六百多家美洲、欧洲和亚洲的厂商参加展览，摊位差不多有两千个。因为这是大型的展览，所以展览的时间特别久，一共六天，时间上的安排跟去年不一样。今年，前四天是专业贸易时间，参观的人都是贸易商和买家，会场里的工作人员忙着介绍新产品，各国的买家和贸易商在一起谈生意，有的谈以后的合作，有的直接下单。但是一般人后两天才可以参观。

虽然那些电子产品都很受大家的欢迎，不过李总经理觉得最特别的是电子书、立体电视和云端科技产品。这次的展览时间很久，让李总经理觉得又忙又累，所以展览一结束就回来了。

(　) 1. 中天科技公司的李总经理去香港

❶参观展览

❷参加展览

❸谈合作的机会

(　) 2. 买家和贸易商参观的时间一共 ❶两天 ❷四天 ❸六天

(　) 3. 那些电子产品

❶只有电子书、立体电视和云端科技产品受大家的欢迎

❷什么产品都受大家的欢迎

❸什么产品也不受大家的欢迎

你怎么说? How Would You Say It?

( ) 1. 工作人员都很忙吧?

( ) 2. 谁都可以参观吗?

( ) 3. 虽然这是大型的展览,

( ) 4. 这次展览有什么特别的新产品?

( ) 5. 李总经理在哪里?

( ) 6. 工作人员忙着介绍新产品。买家和贸易商呢?

A 不过参观的人很少。

B 展览一结束,他就到机场去了。

C 对,谁都很忙。

D 他们,有的忙着谈合作的机会,有的忙着谈生意。

E 都是高科技产品,云端科技产品最特别。

F 有邀请卡的人才可以。

English Translation

Ms. Wang: I heard that you attended an electronics exhibition in Hong Kong last week.

Mr. Li: Yes, I went to a consumer electronics one. I came back yesterday after it ended.

Ms. Wang: How many manufacturers attended?

Mr. Li: There were over 600 in all, including ones from America, Europe and Asia. There were approximately 2,000 booths.

Ms. Wang: Such a large exhibition. Were there any new products that especially stood out?

Mr. Li: Yes, even though there were so many there. I think the e-books, 4D televisions and the products using cloud computing technology stood out the most.

Ms. Wang: Technology advances so quickly. There are more and more high tech products now. How many days did it last all together? Could just anyone attend?

Mr. Li: Six days in total. The first four days were exclusively for businesses and only buyers or business people with invitation cards were allowed to attend. Just the last two days were open to the general public.

Ms. Wang: Since there were so many people on the convention floor, I suppose the people working there were really busy.

Mr. Li: Yes. Everyone was busy demonstrating their products. Buyers and business people from all over the world were there together. Some were talking about future collaboration. Others were placing orders right there on the spot.

工商文化智库 Business-Culture Knowledge Trove

A New Concept of Environmental Protection

Science and technology are constantly advancing. All kinds of new products appear each day in order to make life more convenient, but then end up polluting the environment. Currently, the recycling of disposable products is still not enough to solve the problem of environmental protection. For this reason, more and more countries and businesses are taking the new concept of environmental protection seriously, namely to minimize the use of natural resources and maximize environmental protection through the five stages of product life cycle: from raw materials, manufacturing, sales and consumption to recycling. In view of this, products, such as the electronic information products (basically any product or its accessories which contains or is used in conjunction with electronics) mentioned in the dialog at the beginning of this lesson, should be developed according to these principles.

Green Energy Technology Is the *In* Trend

In the future, key energy resources such as petroleum may slowly dry up. Additionally, when developing industry, commerce, science and technology, the question of how to also protect nature and the environment is an immediate concern. Therefore the trend toward alternative energies such as solar power, wind power, etc. will continue to gain in momentum and dominate the future.

Answer Key

主题词汇 Main Vocabulary

A. 展览、厂商、参加、摊位、会场

B. 工作人员、买家、贸易商、一般人

词语练习 Vocabulary Exercises

1. 一般人 2. 会场 3. 厂商 4. 才 5. 专业

6. 次 7. 结束 8. 人员 9. 特别 10. 下单

重要句型 Sentence Patterns

一、1. 参观的人

2. 联络

二、1. 游戏

2. 护照

三、1. 提高价钱

2. 护照

四、1. 功能

2. 厂商

听力理解 Listening Comprehension

一、1. ❷ 2. ❸

二、1. ❷ 2. ❸

Answer Key

三、

展览内容	展览时间
春季礼品展览	三月八日到三月十二日
食品展览	四月四日到四月十日
电脑展览	五月一日到五月七日
消费电子展览	五月二十四日到五月三十一日

阅读理解 Reading Comprehension

1. ❶ 2. ❷ 3. ❷

你怎么说? How Would You Say It?

1. C 2. F 3. A 4. E 5. B 6. D

听力理解 Listening Comprehension (43)

1

( ) 1. 小林介绍产品不包括什么？

❶外型 ❷价钱 ❸功能

2

( ) 1. 这位小姐先让客人做什么？

❶看护照 ❷填资料 ❸看申请表

3

( ) 1. 这位先生要做什么？

❶刷卡 ❷申请借记卡 ❸存款

4

( ) 1. 礼品是谁送的？

❶总经理 ❷生产立体电视和手机的厂商

❸想和“三资企业”建立关系的公司

( ) 2. 他们为什么送礼？

❶建立关系 ❷要生产 ❸要报告总经理

5

( ) 1. 客人如果要参观展览，礼尚酒店做什么特别的事？

❶订房打八折 ❷免费机场接送

❸让客人免费坐车去会场

(　) 2. 这位先生想什么时候去?

❶现在 ❷还没决定 ❸从3号到9号

6

(　) 1. 为什么小吴要准备?

❶要推出新产品 ❷想让客户更认识产品 ❸客户要参观

(　) 2. 下面哪一句是对的?

❶小吴觉得预算很多 ❷小吴觉得展示室不够

❸经理决定跟总经理说说看

(　) 3. 经理为什么说没办法? 因为

❶没有机会 ❷还没推出新产品 ❸受预算限制

你怎么说? How Would You Say It?

(　) 1. 科技进步得真快。

(　) 2. 这种又轻又薄的手机看起来很时尚。

(　) 3. 您需要开个户头把钱存在我们这儿吗?

(　) 4. 采购礼品的预算减少了，这是怎么一回事?

(　) 5. 今天美元汇价是多少?

A 请稍候。

B 还可以上网和玩游戏。

C 经理的指示很正确。

D 虽然很受年轻人欢迎，不过价钱不便宜。

E 请问，如果要取消订房的话，什么时候通知你们?

( ) 6. 这次展览的前三天是专业贸易时间。 — F 行，没问题。

( ) 7. 请把房间安排在安全门附近。 — G 可不，高科技产品越来越多了。

( ) 8. 智慧型手机的功能除了打电话， — H 总经理指示过年过节不需要送礼了。

( ) 9. 这里是前台，很高兴为您服务。 — I 你的意思是只让有邀请卡的买家参观吗？

( ) 10. 看客户下多少单，再决定送什么礼。 — J 我研究研究以后再决定。

阅读理解 Reading Comprehension

（一）

小胡在一家商务酒店工作，他负责前台的业务，每天安排机场接送客人、订房、入住、退房和取消订房。除了酒店的事，还要和客人建立关系，让他们下次想再来住才行，有的时候算汇价，帮客人兑换人民币，有的时候为了客人采购方便，给客人介绍送礼的礼品。

最近有大型的消费电子展览跟小胡的酒店合作，住在酒店的客人，不但参观展览的费用可以打九折，也能在会场各厂商的摊位免费录影，希望客人喜欢产品就直接下单。因为增加了很多事，小胡更忙更累了；不过，虽然又忙又累，小胡还是觉得很有意思。

(　) 1. 最近小胡的工作怎么样？

❶跟以前一样 ❷增加了很多事 ❸做消费电子展览的事

(　) 2. 前台的业务还包括什么？

❶给客人送礼 ❷帮客人采购 ❸和客人建立关系

(　) 3. 为什么小胡越来越忙？因为

❶除了前台的业务还增加了别的事

❷他觉得很有意思，所以增加了很多事

❸越来越多客人喜欢来住

(　) 4. 消费电子展览为什么跟酒店合作？因为

❶要和客人建立关系

❷希望更多客人来参观

❸要和酒店建立关系

(　) 5. 消费电子展览怎么跟酒店合作？

❶客人在酒店照相、录影

❷客人喜欢就直接下单

❸如果酒店客人参观可以打折

（二）

中天贸易公司业务部的李经理，每年的交际费用比别的经理高很多，不过，业务不比别的经理好，订单也不比别的经理多，所以王总经理想要减少他的交际费用。李经理听说这件事，就马上去见王总经理，他说为了和客户建立很好的关系，他每年三节一定送礼，但是公司采购的礼品，质量不够好，他需要增加一些预算才能买又流行又时尚的礼品，要不然客户可能不下单；至于他平常的应酬也不少，包括请新客户和旧客户吃饭。因为李经理送礼，什么东西都要最好的，所以他申请的交际费用一次比一次高。为了这件事王总经理很不高兴，他觉得送礼是正确的，但是不能超过公司的预算，最后决定取消李经理的交际费用，他还说以后公司送礼的事，直接让公关部门决定就行了。

（ ）1. 王总经理觉得

❶应该要送又流行又时尚的礼品

❷送礼不能超过公司的预算

❸如果业务好的话，送什么礼品都行

（ ）2. 中天贸易公司的王总经理最后

❶减少李经理的交际费用

❷增加李经理的交际费用

❸取消李经理的交际费用

（ ）3. 为什么李经理申请的交际费用一次比一次高？

❶因为他每年三节一定送礼

❷因为他送礼，什么东西都要最好的

❸他的交际费用不受预算的限制

(　) 4. 为什么王总经理不高兴?

❶李经理的业务不好

❷李经理的交际费用太高

❸李经理不常交际应酬

(　) 5. 以后公司送礼的事

❶直接让王总经理决定

❷直接让李经理决定

❸直接让公关部门决定

Please write an essay of 200 or more characters according to the order of the pictures below.

Reference vocabulary and sentence patterns for the short essay assignment:

外型、功能、尺寸、颜色、小、薄、时尚、展览、厂商、参加、摊位、会场、工作人员、买家、贸易商、一般人

……又……又……

……V起来……

……越来越……

虽然……，不过……

……让……

……才……

听力理解 Listening Comprehension

一、1. ❷

二、1. ❸

三、1. ❷

四、1. ❷ 2. ❶

五、1. ❸ 2. ❶

六、1. ❸ 2. ❷ 3. ❸

你怎么说？ How Would You Say It?

1. G 2. D 3. J 4. H 5. A

6. I 7. F 8. B 9. E 10. C

阅读理解 Reading Comprehension

（一）

1. ❷ 2. ❸ 3. ❶ 4. ❷ 5. ❸

（二）

1. ❷ 2. ❸ 3. ❷ 4. ❷ 5. ❸

短文写作 Short Essay

（略）

Lesson *One*

1、A：你好！我叫李明，在工商日报负责采访新闻。这是我的名片，请多指教。

B：不敢当，我是日进贸易公司公关部经理，王大为，负责对外联络的工作，这是我的名片，请多指教。

2、我给你们两位介绍介绍，这位是大中华电视公司新闻部的陈美芳主任，这位是十全食品公司生产部的白文文经理。

Lesson *Two*

1、CA012航班，6点15分飞北京的飞机，请在36号登机口登机。

2、男：白经理您好，一路辛苦了！

女：哪里哪里！王先生，谢谢您来接我。

男：今天晚上我们总经理要在北京楼给您接风。

女：我一来就麻烦大家，真不好意思。

3、CI0912飞纽约的航班，请在26号登机口登机。

AA1203飞北京的航班，10点30分准时起飞。

AC606飞上海的航班，11点35分到达。

Lesson *Three*

1、真有意思，这家饭馆叫北京楼，可招牌菜醉鸡跟红烧鱼，都是上海饭店里有名的菜。

2、吴厂长：李经理，这次贵公司订的货，价钱方面可能要提高才行，因为有些原料涨价了。

李经理：原料涨价了，提高产品的价钱也是没办法的事，可贵厂一定要对质量做最高的要求。

Lesson *Four*

1、白主任今天要到国际会议中心去，可是他的车坏了，所以就打电话叫出租车。他特别告诉出租车公司，要车况好，一流的司机，他才放心。

2、张：李总经理，听说那家饭馆的招牌菜是醉鸡，希望您喜欢。

李：招牌菜怎么能不好吃呢，一定是一流的。不知道坐地铁去行吗？

张：行，打的也行，这儿的出租车车况好，我们打车吧！

Lesson *Five*

1、女：一路辛苦了。怎么样？这次出差，各方面都顺利吧？

男：有小吴这个一流的秘书帮我安排整理一切，怎么可能还有问题呢？

女：可不，他做事，我放心。

2、李总经理：陈秘书，我这礼拜的行程是什么？

秘书：八月十五号　下午3点半　到广州分公司

八月十六号　上午10点　拜访客户

下午4点　跟中友贸易公司谈合作的事

八月十七号	上午9点	坐飞机去上海
	下午2点半	去上海分公司看业务
八月十八号	上午9点	拜访客户
	中午12点	请日进贸易公司吴总吃饭
八月十九号	早上7点	离开上海

Review One

1、男：我们一来就麻烦大家接机，真不好意思。另外，我代表公司谢谢钱总跟各位领导给我们接风，干杯！

2、男：小吴，现在有点儿时间，我们先整理这次出差要拜访的客户名片，你再联络他们。

3、男：希望提高公司的形象，除了要出货准时，还要对质量做最高的要求才行。

女：可不。这样不但产品在市场反应好，客户也能放心下单。

4、男：听说你们中友公司的业务做得很大，分公司不少，都在哪些地方？

女：北方就北京一个地方，南方多一点儿，上海、重庆、广州都有。

男：现在打电话很方便，要不然联络上还真不容易。

女：除了电话联络，有的时候总经理还出差到各分公司去看业务，就是希望领导们都能做好自己负责的工作。

5、女：师傅，我到机场去，要怎么走才快？

男：你要坐飞机还是接客人？

女：美国客户第一次来广州，总经理让我代表公司去接机，我这是第一次接机，心里急着呢！

男：别急，别急，我有我的考量，现在路上车多，要是往右拐，一直走到头，再往左拐，可能快一点儿。

Lesson *Six*

1、客人：服务员，我订房的时候，你们说房间价钱包括早饭，可现在我不舒服，不能下楼，可以请你们送到房间来吗？

前台：房间价钱包括早饭，是您得到楼下吃才行。可您不舒服，怎么能让您下楼呢？如果您愿意的话，另外付一点儿服务费，我们可以给您送。

2、秘书小姐：林经理，您这次出差住的酒店，我已经上网订房了，离国际会议中心不远，要打的、要坐地铁都很方便。

林经理：这次出差，除了我，还有陈总。你订的是单人间还是双人间？

秘书小姐：因为酒店说，这段时间，如果订两个房间的话，可以打七折，所以我就订了两个单人间。

3、总经理：王秘书，我打算三月跟李经理、孙主任到广州出差，我们三天在分公司开会，四天看产品，你帮我们找打折以后最便宜的那段时间订房。

王秘书：好的，总经理。

Lesson Seven

1、秘书：经理，请中友公司吃饭的时间决定了吗？

经理：三月四号晚上6点，在北京楼，是总经理决定的。

秘书：北京楼的菜是一流的，服务也好，费用一定不便宜。

经理：公司有预算的，没问题。

2、男：你们公司的市场比以前更大了，最近一定很忙吧？

女：可不，我们主任指示跟“三资企业”建立关系以后，大家合作得很好，所以现在业务非常忙。

男：嗯，你们主任是正确的，你们公司应该要给他更高的职位、更多的钱才是。

女：是的，总经理常夸奖他，听说他快要做厂长了。

Lesson Eight

1、男：请问，什么人都能在你们银行开户吗？

女：大人都行，小孩儿得有父母帮他填开户申请表。

男：外国人也可以吗？

女：有护照的大人没问题，至于小孩儿，我们研究研究以后再决定。

2、男：公司领导要我采购礼品，费用不少，我想刷卡，可是不能刷，这是怎么回事？

女：你的卡是什么卡？请给我看看。噢，如果要刷这种借记卡的话，你刷卡的费用不能比存款多。

男：你的意思是我户头里的钱不够，所以不能刷卡，是吗？

女：是的，你得再存一些钱在户头里，要不然是不能刷这种卡的。

Lesson Nine

1、王主任：我是展示室的主任，这是下一季要推出的智慧型手机，请您参观。

李先生：谢谢王主任。这些手机看起来很时尚，不知道有什么功能？

王主任：功能很多，除了打电话，还可以照相、录影、上网、玩游戏和看电影。

2、智慧型手机的功能越来越多，差不多跟小型电脑一样。至于颜色，我们什么颜色都有，但是银色、黑色和红色，是最受年轻人欢迎的。

3、这是中友科技公司上个月刚推出的新产品。第一个产品是十八吋的笔记型电脑，外型又轻又好看，颜色是年轻人最喜欢的银色，价钱要美金一千九百九十九元；第二个产品是红色的新型手机，外型又小又薄，非常小，只有两吋，价钱只要美金一千二百元；第三个产品是六十五吋的大型电视，外型很时尚，价钱是美金三千三百五十元。市场的反应都很不错。价钱不贵，年轻人都很喜欢。

Lesson Ten

1、工作人员：先生，请你把邀请卡给我看看。

王先生：什么邀请卡？

工作人员：今天是专业贸易时间，我们只让有邀请卡的买家或贸易商参观。

王先生：对不起，我没有邀请卡。

工作人员：没有邀请卡的人，明天才可以参观。

2、今年我去香港参加消费电子展览，一共有五天，虽然参加展览的厂商和摊位比去年少，不过有很多高科技产品。我觉得今年最特别的是有不少智慧型手机、电子书、立体电视和云端科技产品，这些都很受各国买家和贸易商的欢迎。

3、这是今年北京春季商业展览表，一共有四个展览。从三月八日到三月十二日有春季礼品展览，四月的展览是食品展览，展览时间从四月四日到四月十日；五月的展览有两次，一次是从五月一日到五月七日的电脑展览，还有一次是五月二十四日到五月三十一日的消费电子展览。

Review *Two*

1、男：小林，请你把下一季要推出产品的尺寸、颜色、功能放在网络上，给客户介绍介绍，至于价钱，得看客户反应再决定。

2、女：申请借记卡跟申请信用卡一样，不但需要看您的护照，也得填一些资料，这是申请表，请您先过目。

3、男：刷借记卡的时候，得受户头里存款的限制，不太方便，我研究研究以后再决定要不要申请。

4、女：为什么有这么多礼品？

男：报告总经理，这是深圳的一些“三资企业”送来的，他们想和我们公司建立关系。

女：他们是做什么的？

男：有的生产立体电视，有的生产智慧型手机。

5、女：下午好，这里是前台，很高兴为您服务。

男：听说从3号到9号这段时间有电子产品展览，住在你们礼尚酒店的客人如果要参观的话，可以打折，是吗？

女：是的，参观的费用打八折，去会场我们还有车免费接送。您打算什么时候去？

男：这就去，行吗？

女：没问题，请您到前台来。

6、男：小吴，下午三点，从香港来的客户要参观我们的展示室，请你准备准备。

女：经理，为了让客户更认识我们的产品，是不是可以增加一个展示室？要不然东西太多了。

男：虽然你说的很正确，不过，公司预算就这么多，现在没办法增加。

女：下一季再推出新产品的时候，您可以跟总经理说说看。

男：那得看有机会没有。

Vocabulary Index

生词索引表

A				
ānpái	安排	安排	to arrange; plan	5
ānquánmén	安全门	安全門	safety exit	6
B				
bǎ	把	把	grammatical word used to place the object before the verb	8
bàifǎng	拜访	拜訪	to visit; to call on	5
bāokuò	包括	包括	to include	6
báo	薄	薄	thin (said of things)	9
bàogào	报告	報告	to report	7
bǐ	比	比	compared to	7
biǎo	表	表	table, list	5
búguò	不过	不過	however	7
bù gǎn dāng	不敢当	不敢當	(I) don't dare accept (your compliment)	1
bùmén	部门	部門	department	1
C				
cǎifǎng	采访	採訪	to interview; to gather news	1
cǎigòu	采购	採購	to purchase	7
cānguān	参观	參觀	to visit	9
cānjiā	参加	參加	to attend	10
chǎnpǐn	产品	產品	product	1
chǎngshāng	厂商	廠商	business; firm; manufacturer	10
chǎngzhǎng	厂长	廠長	factory director	3
chāoguò	超过	超過	to go over, to exceed	8
chēkuàng	车况	車況	condition (of a vehicle)	4
chēxíng	车型	車型	model (of car)	4

chǐcùn	尺寸	尺寸	size; measurement	9
chūchāi	出差	出差	to go on business travel	5
chūhuò	出货	出貨	to produce or manufacture goods; to deliver goods	3
chūzūchē	出租车	出租車	taxi	4
chuánzhēn	传真	傳真	to fax	6
cì	次	次	time (as in 'this time')	10
cún	存	存	to store, to deposit; to exist	8
cúnkuǎn	存款	存款	to deposit (money)	8
cùn	吋	吋	(English) inch	9
D				
dǎchē	打车	打車	to take a taxi	4
dǎdī	打的	打的	to take a taxi	4
dǎ fāpiào	打发票	打發票	to give a receipt	4
dǎzhé	打折	打折	to give a discount	6
dài	带	帶	to take	5
dàibiǎo	代表	代表	to represent	2
dān	单	單	piece of paper (as in a receipt, etc.)	8
dānrénjiān	单人间	單人間	single room	6
dàodá	到达	到達	to reach or arrive at (a destination)	2
dēngjī	登机	登機	to board (an airplane)	2
dìtiě	地铁	地鐵	subway; metro	4
diǎn(cài)	点(菜)	點(菜)	to order (a dish)	3
diànzǐ	电子	電子	electronic; an electron	10
dìng	订	訂	to place an order (for merchandise)	3
dìngfáng	订房	訂房	to book or reserve a room	6
duàn	段	段	period (of time); section	6
duìhuàn	兑换	兌換	to exchange money	8
duìle	对了	對了	Oh, that's right.; correct, right	5

F				
fǎnyìng	反应	反應	reaction	5
fāngmiàn	方面	方面	aspect	3
fèiyong	费用	費用	fee; cost; expense	7
fengōngsī	分公司	分公司	branch office	5
fúwùfèi	服务费	服務費	service fee	6
fúwùyuán	服务员	服務員	waiter; waitress; service person	3
fù	付	付	to pay	4
fùzé	负责	負責	to be responsible for	1
G				
gānbēi	干杯	乾杯	to dry one's glass (usually said when drinking alcohol)	3
gè	各	各	each	3
gèng	更	更	still; yet; more	7
gōngguān	公关	公關	public relations	1
gōngnéng	功能	功能	function	9
gōngzuò	工作	工作	to work; a job (or jobs)	1
guǎi	拐	拐	to turn	4
guò	过	過	to celebrate (usually used with Chinese New Year, major festivals and birthdays)	7
guòmù	过目	過目	to take a look at	5
H				
hángbān	航班	航班	(airline) flight	2
hángyuán	行员	行員	(bank) teller	8
hézuò	合作	合作	to work together; to cooperate	1
hēisè	黑色	黑色	the color black	9
hóngshāo	红烧	紅燒	to braise in soy sauce	3
hùtóu	户头	戶頭	(bank) account	8
hùzhào	护照	護照	passport	8

huānyíng	欢迎	歡迎	to welcome	2
huìchǎng	会场	會場	meeting place	10
huìjià	汇价	匯價	exchange rate	8
huò	或	或	or	10
J				
jīchǎng	机场	機場	airport	2
jīhuì	机会	機會	chance, opportunity	1
jì	季	季	season (of the year)	9
jìzhě	记者	記者	reporter	1
jiàqián	价钱	價錢	price	3
jiǎnshǎo	减少	減少	to decrease	7
jiànlì	建立	建立	to establish	7
jiāojì	交际	交際	social interaction	7
jiē	接	接	to meet (someone); to pick someone up	2
jiēfēng	接风	接風	to receive visitors	2
jiējī	接机	接機	to meet someone at / pick up someone from the airport	2
jiéshù	结束	結束	to conclude; to end	10
jièjìkǎ	借记卡	借記卡	debit card	8
jìnbù	进步	進步	to advance, to make progress	10
jīnglǐ	经理	經理	manager	1
juédìng	决定	決定	to decide	7
K				
kāi	开	開	to open	8
kǎoliang	考量	考量	consideration	4
kěbù	可不	可不	Isn't it though?; That's right.	4
kèhù	客户	客戶	customer; client	5
kuājiǎng	夸奖	誇獎	to praise	5
L				

lǐpǐn	礼品	禮品	gift; present	7
liánluò	联络	聯絡	to contact	1
liǎojiě	了解	了解	to understand	5
lǐngdǎo	领导	領導	leadership; guide	3
lìngwài	另外	另外	in addition; also	5
liúxíng	流行	流行	popular	9
lùyǐng	录影	錄影	to record video	9
M				
mǎijiā	买家	買家	buyer (for a company)	10
máng bú guòlái	忙不过来	忙不過來	to be too busy to handle	5
màoyì	贸易	貿易	trade; business	10
màoyìshāng	贸易商	貿易商	trader (also importer / exporter)	10
mìshū	秘书	祕書	secretary; office assistant	5
miǎnfèi	免费	免費	free of charge	6
míngpiàn	名片	名片	business card	1
N				
nǎlǐ	哪里	哪裡	Where? (also used as polite way of turning down a compliment)	1
niánqīngrén	年轻人	年輕人	young people	9
P				
páizi	牌子	牌子	sign (in front of a store)	8
Q				
qǐfēi	起飞	起飛	to take off (said of aircraft)	2
qiántái	前台	前檯	front desk	6
qīng	轻	輕	light	9
qǐng shāohòu	请稍候	請稍候	Please wait a moment.	6
qǔkuǎn	取款	取款	to withdraw (money)	8
qǔxiāo	取消	取消	to cancel	6
R				

ràng	让	讓	to let, to allow	4
rényuán	人员	人員	personnel	10
rènshi	认识	認識	to know	1
rùguān	入关	入關	to enter customs (e.g. at an airport)	2
rùzhù	入住	入住	to check in (to a hotel room, etc.)	6
S				
shàngcài	上菜	上菜	to bring food to the table	3
shàngwǎng	上网	上網	to get on-line, to get on the Internet	6
shēnqǐng	申请	申請	to apply	8
shēngchǎn	生产	生產	to produce	1
shīfu	师傅	師傅	used to address service workers	4
shíshàng	时尚	時尚	stylish	9
shōuxià	收下	收下	to accept or receive	2
shǒujī	手机	手機	mobile phone; cellphone	9
shòu	受	受	to receive	8
shuākǎ	刷卡	刷卡	to use a credit card or debit card *(literally: to swipe a card)*	8
shuāngrénjiān	双人间	雙人間	double room	6
shùnlì	顺利	順利	smooth; without encountering problems	2
sījī	司机	司機	driver	4
sòng	送	送	to take (someone to someplace); to escort	2
sònglǐ	送礼	送禮	to give a gift	7
suàn	算	算	to calculate	6
suīrán	虽然	雖然	despite; in spite of; although	10
T				
tānwèi	摊位	攤位	exhibition booth	10
tán	谈	談	to speak or chat about	3
tèbié	特别	特別	special; unusual	10

tígāo	提高	提高	to raise; to increase	3
tián	填	填	to fill out (a form)	8
tōngzhī	通知	通知	to inform	5
tǒngyī	统一	統一	united	4
tuīchū	推出	推出	to release to the public (said of products, books, etc.)	9
tuìfáng	退房	退房	to check out (of a hotel room, etc.)	6
W				
wàixíng	外型	外型	(external) appearance	9
wányóuxì	玩游戏	玩遊戲	to play games	9
wǎngluò	网络	網絡	the Internet	6
wèile	为了	為了	for; in order to	7
X				
xiàdān	下单	下單	to place an order	4
xiànjīn	现金	現金	cash	8
xiànzhì	限制	限制	limit; limitation	8
xìnyòngkǎ	信用卡	信用卡	credit card	6
xíng	行	行	to be okay, to be acceptable	3
xíng	型	型	model; type	9
xíngchéng	行程	行程	travel itinerary	5
xíngli	行李	行李	luggage	2
xíngxiàng	形象	形象	image	4
xūyào	需要	需要	to need; to want; to require	7
Y				
yánjiū	研究	研究	to discuss; to think over	7
yāoqǐngkǎ	邀请卡	邀請卡	invitation card	10
yāoqiú	要求	要求	requirement; request; demand	3
yàobùrán	要不然	要不然	otherwise	5
yèwù	业务	業務	professional work; business	5
yīliú	一流	一流	first-rate; of the best quality	4

yílù xīnkǔ	一路辛苦	一路辛苦	a hard or difficult journey	2
yíqiè	一切	一切	everything	2
yìbānrén	一般人	一般人	normal people; the average person	10
yínsè	银色	銀色	the color light gray	9
yìngchou	应酬	應酬	to entertain (guests)	7
yùsuàn	预算	預算	budget	7
yuán	元	元	unit of money	6
yuánliào	原料	原料	raw material(s)	3
yuè lai yuè	越来越	越來越	more and more	9
Z				
zēngjiā	增加	增加	to increase	7
zhǎnlǎn	展览	展覽	exhibition; display	10
zhǎnshìshì	展示室	展示室	showroom	9
zhǎngjià	涨价	漲價	to rise in price	3
zhànghù	帐户	帳戶	(bank) account	8
zhāopaicài	招牌菜	招牌菜	specialty (dish)	3
zhāoshǒu	招手	招手	to wave one’s hand(s)	4
zhékòu	折扣	折扣	discount	6
zhěnglǐ	整理	整理	to arrange, to put in order	5
zhèngquè	正确	正確	correct; accurate	7
zhī	支	支	measure word for mobile phones; branch, twig	9
zhīpiào	支票	支票	(bank) check	8
zhíjiē	直接	直接	directly	10
zhíwèi	职位	職位	position (within a company)	1
zhǐjiào	指教	指教	please give advice	1
zhǐshì	指示	指示	to point out	7
zhìliàng	质量	質量	quality	3
zhìyú	至于	至於	as far as; concerning; to go as far as to	6

zhòng	重	重	heavy	9
zhǔrèn	主任	主任	director, chair	1
zhǔyi	主意	主意	idea; plan	4
zhǔnshí	准时	準時	to be on time, punctual	2
zhuānyè	专业	專業	professional; specialized	10
zǒngjīnglǐ	总经理	總經理	general manager	2
zuì	醉	醉	drunk	3

Specialized Terms Index

专有名词索引表

Pinyin	Simplified Characters	Traditional Characters	English	Lesson
Běijīng Lóu	北京楼	北京樓	Peking Garden Restaurant	2
Běijīng Shǒudū Jīchǎng	北京首都机场	北京首都機場	Beijing Capital Airport	2
Chóngqìng	重庆	重慶	city name	5
Dàzhōnghuá Diànshì Gōngsī	大中华电视公司	大中華電視公司	Dazhonghua Television (company)	1
Gōngshāng Rìbào	工商日报	工商日報	Commercial Daily (newspaper)	1
Guǎngzhōu	广州	廣州	city name	5
Guójì Huìyì Zhōngxīn	国际会议中心	國際會議中心	International Convention Center	4
Hú Sī	胡思	胡思	person's name	6
Huángpǔ Jiāng	黄浦江	黃浦江	Huangpu River	4
Jīn Ān Diànnǎo Gōngsī	金安电脑公司	金安電腦公司	Jin An Computer Company	2
Lǐ Míng	李明	李明	person's name	1
Lǐ Rén	李仁	李仁	person's name	2
Lǐyáng Shāngwù Jiǔdiàn	里洋商务酒店	里洋商務酒店	hotel name	6
Lín Lì	林利	林利	person's name	6
Měizhōu	美洲	美洲	the Americas	10
Niǔyuē Kěnnídí Jīchǎng	纽约肯尼迪机场	紐約肯尼迪機場	New York Kennedy Airport	2
Ōuzhōu	欧洲	歐洲	Europe	10

Rì Jìn Màoyì Gōngsī	日进贸易公司	日進貿易公司	Ri Jin Trading (company)	1
Shànghǎi Fàndiàn	上海饭店	上海飯店	The Shanghai Hotel	3
Shēnzhèn	深圳	深圳	city in Southern China	7
Shíquán Shípǐn Gōngsī	十全食品公司	十全食品公司	Perfect Foods (company)	1
Shǐdífū	史迪夫	史迪夫	Steve (transliteration)	8
Wàitān	外滩	外灘	the Bund	4
Wáng Dàwéi	王大为	王大為	person's name	1
Wǔhàn	武汉	武漢	city name	5
Xiānggǎng	香港	香港	Hong Kong	10
Yàzhōu	亚洲	亞洲	Asia	10
Zhōng Yǒu Kējì Gōngsī	中友科技公司	中友科技公司	Zhong You Science and Technology Company	2

Practical Vocabulary Index

实用名词索引表

Pinyin	Simplified Characters	Traditional Characters	English	Lesson
bǐjìxíng diànnǎo	笔记型电脑	筆記型電腦	notebook (computer)	9
Chūn Jié	春节	春節	Spring Festival	7
diànzǐ shū	电子书	電子書	e-book	10
Duānwǔ Jié	端午节	端午節	Dragon Boat Festival	7
hóngshāo yú	红烧鱼	紅燒魚	red-braised fish	3
kāihù shēnqǐngbiǎo	开户申请表	開戶申請表	application for opening an account	8
lìtǐ diànshì	立体电视	立體電視	4D television	10
Měiyuán	美元	美元	U.S. Dollar	8
Ōuyuán	欧元	歐元	Euro	8
Rénmínbì	人民币	人民幣	Renminbi (aka Chinese Yuan)	8
Rìbì	日币	日幣	Japanese Yen	8
sānzī qǐyè	三资企业	三資企業	Refers to the three types of companies which are funded or operated according to one of the three ways foreign investment and foreign management are allowed in China under Chinese law, namely: 1. Chinese-foreign equity joint ventures, 2. Chinese-foreign contractual joint ventures or 3. wholly foreign-owned enterprises.	7

shànghǎi cài	上海菜	上海菜	Shanghainese Cuisine	3
shàoxīng jiǔ	绍兴酒	紹興酒	Shaoxing rice wine	3
shùmǎ xiàngjī	数码相机	數碼相機	digital camera	9
xiāofèi diànzǐ zhǎnlǎn	消费电子展览	消費電子展覽	consumer electronics exhibition	10
Yīngbàng	英镑	英鎊	British Pound	8
yúnduān kējì chǎnpǐn	云端科技产品	雲端科技產品	cloud computing technology products	10
zhìhuìxíng shǒujī	智慧型手机	智慧型手機	smart phone	9
Zhōngqiū Jié	中秋节	中秋節	Mid-Autumn Festival	7
zuìjī	醉鸡	醉雞	wine-steeped chicken (also called drunken chicken)	3

Sentence Pattern List

句型索引表

Pinyin	Patterns Point	Lesson
ba	吧	10
búdàn……yě……	不但……也……	4
……cái……	……才……	10
chúle……hái……	除了……还……	5
děikàn……	得看……	6
……fāngmiàn	……方面	3
Fēijī time cóng place qǐfēi, hángbān time dàodá.	飞机 time 从 place 起飞，航班 time 到达。	2
jiùxiàng NP yíyàng	就像 NP 一样	4
lái + (Nu) + M + N	来 + (Nu) + M + N	3
N_1 bǐ N_2 SV	N_1 比 N_2 SV	7
qǐngduō V	请多 V	1
ràng	让	10
rúguǒ……dehuà	如果……的话	6
……shàng	……上	5
S bǎ O V zài PW	（S）把 O V 在 PW	8
S bǎ O V zhe	S 把 O V 着	8
S (bú) shòu……xiànzhì	S（不）受……限制	8
S shénme O dōu V……	S 什么 O 都 V……	3
S_1 yì V_1O_1……(S_1) / S_2 jiù V_2O_2	S_1 一 V_1O_1 …… (S_1) / S_2 就 V_2O_2	2
S zài……bùmén fùzé……de gōngzuò.	S 在……部门负责……的工作。	1
suīrán……, búguò……	虽然……，不过……	10
VV kàn	VV 看	9
……V qilai……	……V 起来……	9

V zhe	V 着	5
wèile……	为了……	7
xīwàng yǐhòu + Clause	希望以后 + Clause	1
S_1 xiān V_1O_1, (S_1) / S_2 zài V_2O_2	S_1 先 V_1O_1，(S_1) / S_2 再 V_2O_2	2
yào……cái……	要……才……	3
yàobùrán……	要不然……	5
……yěxíng, ……yěxíng.	Q：……？ A：……也行，……也行。	4
yòu……yòu……	……又……又……	9
yuè lai yuè……	越来越……	9
Zěnme néng ràng……ne?	怎么能让……呢？	4
zhèjiù……	这就……	7
zhìyú	至于	6

Vocabulary Differences between Taiwan and Mainland China

两岸词汇差异对照表

中国大陆说法		台灣說法		Lesson
chūzūchē	出租车	jìchéngchē	計程車	4
dădī / dăchē / zuò chūzūchē	打的 / 打车 / 坐出租车	zuò jìchéngchē	坐計程車	4
dă fāpiào / kāi fāpiào	打发票 / 开发票	kāi shōujù	開收據	4
dēngjīkǒu	登机口	dēngjīmén	登機門	2
dìtiě	地铁	jiéyùn	捷運	4
diànnăo / jìsuànjī	电脑/计算机	diànnăo	電腦	9
fúwùyuán	服务员	fúwùshēng	服務生	3
huìjià	汇价	huìlǜ	匯率	8
jìdù	季度	jì	季	9
jièjìkă	借记卡	visa jīnróngkă	visa金融卡	8
lǐngdăo	领导	gànbù / zhǔguăn	幹部 / 主管	3
lùyǐng / lùxiàng	录影/录像	lùyǐng	錄影	9
Niǔyuē Kěnnídí Jīchăng	纽约肯尼迪机场	Niǔyuē Gānnăidí Jīchăng	紐約甘迺迪機場	2
páizi	牌子	páigào	牌告	8
qiántái	前台	guìtái	櫃台	6
shāngwù jiǔdiàn	商务酒店	shāngwù lǚguăn / shāngwù fàndiàn	商務旅館 / 商務飯店	6
shùmă xiàngjī	数码相机	shùwèi xiàngjī	數位相機	9
wăngluò	网络	wănglù	網路	6
xìnxī	信息	zīxùn / xùnxí	資訊 / 訊息	1
zhìliàng	质量	pǐnzhí	品質	3

Abbreviations List

词类略语表

Adv	Adverb	副词
Conj	Conjunction	连词
CV	Coverb	前置介词
Dem	Demonstrative Pronoun	指示代词
IE	Idiomatic Expression	习惯用语
M	Measure	量词
N	Noun	名词
NP	Noun Phrase	名词短语
Nu	Number	数词
O	Object	宾语
PT	Pattern	句型
PW	Place Word	处所词
QW	Question Word	疑问词
RC	Resultative Compound	结果复合动词
S	Subject	主语
SV	Stative Verb	性状动词
V	Verb	动词
VO	Verb Object Compound	动宾复合词

Picture Credits
达志影像提供：
P.39, 41, 64, 105, 148